T0208925

Moments of
FOCUS

A Weekly Devotional, Journal &
Bible Study Leader's Support Guide

BeNeca Griffin

WESTBOW
PRESS®
A DIVISION OF THOMAS NELSON
& ZONDERVAN

WestBow Press books may be ordered through booksellers or by contacting:

WestBow Press
A Division of Thomas Nelson & Zondervan
1663 Liberty Drive
Bloomington, IN 47403
www.westbowpress.com
1 (866) 928-1240

Because of the dynamic nature of the Internet, any web addresses or links contained in this book may have changed since publication and may no longer be valid. The views expressed in this work are solely those of the author and do not necessarily reflect the views of the publisher, and the publisher hereby disclaims any responsibility for them.

Any people depicted in stock imagery provided by Getty Images are models, and such images are being used for illustrative purposes only.
Certain stock imagery © Getty Images.

ISBN: 978-1-9736-9512-7 (sc)
ISBN: 978-1-9736-9513-4 (hc)
ISBN: 978-1-9736-9511-0 (e)

Library of Congress Control Number: 2020911731

Print information available on the last page.

WestBow Press rev. date: 7/22/2020

Contents

Acknowledgments

Thank You, God, for gifting me with the ability to share in the delivery of Your Word through Your moments of focus. It has absolutely been my joy to share with others as you have shared with me.

Thank you, Clarence, for being the best hubby and sounding board this girl could have. Your love and support have been incredible in ways that can never be articulated.

To my girls, or the young women of my tribe—Aaliyah, Alani, Tiyanane, and DeNoire—I love you and truly appreciate the reflection of greatness that each of you add to my life.

Rhonda Rochelle, I cannot thank you enough for encouraging me to share this "batter" at the next level and for contributing your gifts to this project. DeNoire, thank you for your insight and contributions to the shaping of this work.

Will, Sukari, Mom, Anisa, Briggette, Vanessa, Dawn, Delmar, Kristen, PJ, Francine and Kathy I thank you for your support on this project.

Introduction

Moments of Focus is a Weekly Devotional, Journal & Bible Study Leader's Support Guide. It provides clarity for individuals who are looking for a better understanding of how the Word of GOD applies to their lives personally. The journal component guides you on how to empty your thoughts into your conversations with God. It allows you to connect and create personal action plans that can move your life forward instantly. It also provides 52 weeks of content including weekly topics, lessons and scriptures that can be used as foundational points for Bible Study Leaders (Pastors, Priests, & Small Group Leaders) for sermons, homilies and weekly sessions.

This book will assist you as you make time to sit with God every week and reflect on the ways in which you should grow and move forward into the life that He has designed for you. It will help you outline your personal thoughts about yourself and your steps ahead. It will help you to draw the parallels between many things that God said centuries ago and what He is saying today.

Built in is a guided framework that will bring you closer to God by enhancing your conversations, highlighting new and exciting directives that He has for you and uncovering those things that you need to change. It will invoke movement in your life that will serve as a great blessing for you and those He places around you.

I am sharing 52 of the Moments of Focus that God shared with me as He guided me into my purpose. His words provided me with an instant sense of clarity about how to handle the situations that were happening in my life. Every week, they served as a guided tour that helped me get through the week with direction.

These moments taught me about the consistency of His Word. I believe that God will use these Moments of Focus to help you set the framework for connecting with many areas of God's Word and deepen your relationship with Him through your conversations in journaling and guided prayer.

Dear heavenly Father,

Thank You for providing me with moments of focused time to sit with You every week and reflect on the ways in which I should grow and move forward into the life that You have designed for me.

I realize that this time will bring us closer together, enhance our conversations, and uncover some things that I need to change, as well as highlight new and exciting directives that You have for my life. I pray that this process will invoke movement in my life that will be a great blessing for me and those You place me with.

As I work through these moments with You, I will take notes on the changes that I both need and want to make as well as those things I should do differently. I will empty my thoughts into my conversations with You and make room for Your directions. I pray that this entire process will cause the changes in my life that are needed, making me complete according to Your will.

1

Make Your Reservations, and God Will Buy Your Ticket

I'm sure about this: the one who started a good work in you will stay with you to complete the job by the day of Christ Jesus.
—PHILIPPIANS 1:6 (CEV)

We often postpone outlining the ideas that are associated with our purposes, dreams, and the visions that God has given us until we feel as though we have enough money to finance our plans. We often worry and wait on a financial confirmation before giving ourselves permission to move forward. The reality is that money is never the determining factor on whether we are able to move to the next step but rather a tool that the enemy uses to prevent us from doing something that God has already given us the desire and confirmation to do. If God gives us the situation, the money will come! When God has somewhere for us to go, all we have to do is commit to taking the trip and make the reservation (or take a step toward His will for our lives). He will take care of the costs involved and see us through. Whether we are writing a book, starting a business, or whatever we are led to do, when God plants a seed in our hearts and confirms that it is the right path for our lives, He will always complete the final step of making sure that everything is paid for. Most parents don't give their children their college tuition until the child has actually applied to college, written out their plans for success, and are clear on their very next step. We must apply ourselves to our purposes, prepare our plans for success, make a reservation for our very next step, and trust that God will take care of the costs.

What's the Focus?

Stop waiting on money to start your plans.
Success follows plans that have been activated by preparation.

Journal Questions:

- What visions or assignments has God given to you?

_____

_____

_____

_____

_____

_____

_____

_____

_____

_____

- What are you not preparing for in your life because of a lack of finances?

_____

_____

_____

_____

_____

_____

_____

_____

_____

_____

- What bags can you pack now for your trip? What can you do now to be better prepared for where you're going?

_____

_____

_____

_____

_____

_____

_____

_____

_____

_____

Prayer: Dear heavenly Father, please help me to focus on the portion of the work You have given me to complete on behalf of Your purpose. Please help me to understand that it is not my responsibility to know all that You know about how things will be put together and paid for. Yet it is my responsibility to focus on and complete what I can understand—knowing by faith that You will make sure everything is completed.

2

Is It Harder to Sit Still in a Moment of Patience or Walk on a Rocky Road?

*If you do what the Lord wants, He will make
certain each step you take is sure.*
—PSALM 37:23 (CEV)

Time and time again we ask God to go before us and order our steps to better our courses in life. However, we don't always choose to wait until God is finished paving the road before taking our next steps.

At times, God will reveal something to us that He has prepared for our lives *before* He has removed the obstacles and put everything into place. Because of this, we often get excited about the promise but then discouraged about the process and the time that it may take. At times, we're in such a rush that we will try to go around Him and bypass His process in an effort to move things forward in our lives.

When we decide to walk on an unpaved road, it affects not only the destination but also the journey. After moving ahead on our own, because most dirt roads look alike, we tend to get frustrated, stop, and just give up because we don't know which way to go. We sometimes find ourselves in the middle of nowhere crying out to God, asking Him to show us the direction that we chose not to wait on.

How can we be clear on which way to travel if we do not wait on God to move the obstacles out of our paths and smooth out the road ahead? When God orders our steps, no matter what we have to go through,

He will prepare us for the journey if we listen. Walking on gravel and dirt when we're not prepared and don't have on the right shoes will make the journey more uncomfortable than it has to be. Waiting on God allows us to travel on the smooth pavement that He has prepared. We must train our minds to sit still in moments of patience as we mentally, physically, and spiritually prepare for our next steps.

What's the Focus?

Although it can be hard to wait on God,
you will always be more successful traveling
with His direction than without it.

Journal Questions:

- What areas of your life have you moved into or what decisions have you made without God's direction?

_____

_____

_____

_____

_____

_____

_____

_____

_____

_____

- What has it cost you to start over and get back on track with God?

_____
_____
_____
_____
_____
_____
_____
_____
_____
_____

- In order to move forward, what specific answers do you need from God about your next steps?

_____
_____
_____
_____
_____
_____
_____
_____
_____
_____

Prayer: Dear heavenly Father, please help me to follow Your direction, even when I don't understand the road map. Place my feet step by step according to Your will. Please help me to sit still in the quiet moments, giving praise and thanks for all that I know You are doing during the times when I do not hear Your voice.

3

Walk through the Door and See Who's There to Help You— It May Not Be Who You Think

With all your heart you must trust the Lord
and not your own judgment.
—PROVERBS 3:5 (CEV)

We tend to use the words *supposed to* too often. When a meteorologist predicts it will rain and it doesn't, we say, "It was supposed to rain." The truth is that it was *not* supposed to rain because God did not order it so.

Sometimes we ask God to guide us along our way but then get upset when people *we* wanted to help us didn't do what *we* thought they should have based on the nature of the relationship we have with them (e.g., family or friends). Once we ask God to order our steps, He is then in full control and in charge of what is supposed to happen. He will decide whom He wants to use to help us. However, we often keep distractions in our lives that prevent us from being able to listen and really hear messages from God. Most people in our lives are not sent to us so that we can have everyday conversations with them. Most people, if we stay prayerful, will bring us a part of our puzzle. When we allow God to bring people into our lives for His purpose, those people will come with a message. When we have unnecessary conversations with everyone who comes our way, it's hard to hear the message because of the extra words. Most of us encounter times when we just need to talk to someone. However, we have to remember to save our most important conversations for the times when we are speaking with God. When we ask someone to provide for us and he or she steps in as our resource, God doesn't always get the glory He deserves. The person we asked gets most of the praise. Sometimes God will tie the hands of those we think are supposed to do something for us, causing us to see clearly that we need to depend on Him and His methods.

What's the Focus?

Don't get upset with people when they don't do what you
think they are able or supposed to do. Trust that God
has His reasons for using the methods He chooses.

Journal Questions:

- Are you waiting to get help from someone whom God has not ordered to help you?

_____

_____

_____

_____

_____

_____

_____

_____

_____

_____

- Is there someone you are refusing help from because he or she is not whom you think should be helping you?

_____
_____
_____
_____
_____
_____
_____
_____
_____

- In what areas of your life will you relinquish full control to God?

_____
_____
_____
_____
_____
_____
_____
_____

Prayer: Dear heavenly Father, please help me focus on my trust and belief in You and Your methods. Help me to appreciate every move that You approve toward the completion of the assignments that You give me, regardless of my understanding. Please bless me to have the discernment to know Your approved way. Guide me to greatness according to Your will.

4

Sometimes It Takes a Tornado to Move Us to the Right Location

You planned something bad for me, but God produced something good from it, in order to save the lives of many people, just as he's doing today.
—GENESIS 50:20 (CEV)

At times when we are going through a storm, or time of trouble, our first response is to say that the devil is trying to destroy our lives. This may very well be true, but we have to remember that, when we are connected to God, nothing happens to us that God does not allow.

The old saying "What the devil means for bad, God means for good" addresses the fact that God will not allow us to go through something for no reason. It is easier for us to blame our trials solely on our enemy than to accept that God is actually allowing us to experience something that will allow for growth in our lives or move us to another location. Sometimes, when God tries to teach us something quietly, we don't listen or we choose to ignore Him. Because of this, we are at times forced to go through the wind of what seems to be a tornado and are carried to our next step. Tornadoes come with audible warning signs. Most people say that they sound like a train coming near. It is important that we take the time to listen and walk according to His direction so that God does not have to send the train to take us where He needs us to be. When we find ourselves in the middle of a tornado, we must remember that He will always protect us and that it is never too late to pray and listen, understanding that it is not God's intention to destroy us but to make us better.

What's the Focus?

God will move you to save your life and
position you within your purpose.

Journal Questions:

- In what areas of your life has God moved your circumstances in order to move *you*?

_____

_____

_____

_____

_____

_____

_____

_____

_____

- What were the warning signs before the wind?

_____

_____

_____

_____

_____

_____

_____

_____

_____

- What is God telling you to do right now?

_____

_____

_____

_____

_____

_____

_____

_____

_____

_____

Prayer: Dear heavenly Father, please help me to hear Your voice when making decisions. God, please remind me that, when I find myself in situations that seem to come with heavy wind and rain, You are always in control and You can produce something amazing to save and better my life.

5

Are You Pressing the Snooze Button on Your Alarm Clock with God?

There is a right time for everything.
—ECCLESIASTES 3:1 (ERV)

Is there something that God has put on your heart to do (to write, to create, to design, to teach, to produce) that you are taking your time with? Do you find yourself waiting on Him to wake you up again to remind you to get it started or finished? It's important to understand that when God shares His vision with us and gives us an opportunity to participate in something that He has planned, the opportunity is for an appointed time. We should be mindful not to miss this specific time to work for and with Him.

If we press our snooze button in the mornings too many times and are late to work, we will be replaced. The same thing applies with the jobs that God has for us to complete. It would be terrible to be replaced for sleeping in on the job. God will have His plans finished, even if He has someone else complete them.

What's the Focus?

Don't assume that you have extra time to
get God's assignments done.

Journal Questions:

- What has God assigned you to do?

_____

_____

_____

_____

_____

_____

_____

_____

_____

- What part of your assignment are you sleeping on or taking your time with?

_____

_____

_____

_____

_____

_____

_____

_____

_____

_____

- What part of your assignment can you move forward today to be closer to completing your work with God?

_____

_____

_____

_____

_____

_____

_____

_____

_____

_____

Prayer: Dear heavenly Father, please help me to be focused on the timing of Your assignments. Help me see the importance of the people that it serves. Help me to stay connected to the greatness of Your direction.

6

What Kind of Fruit Do People Pick from You?

A good tree cannot produce bad fruit, and a bad tree
cannot produce good fruit. You can tell what a tree is like
by the fruit it produces. You cannot pick figs or grapes from
thornbushes. Good people do good things because of the
good in their hearts. Bad people do bad things because of the
evil in their hearts. Your words show what is in your heart.
—LUKE 6:43–45 (CEV)

Do not let any unwholesome talk come out of your mouths,
but only what is helpful for building others up according
to their needs, that it may benefit those who listen.
—EPHESIANS 4:29 (NIV)

There's an old saying from the Bible that states that you can tell a tree by the fruit that it bears. This means that you can tell who someone is by what they produce, say, or do.

There are moments in our lives when we feel that we need to learn more about ourselves and gain a clearer reflection of who we are. One way to do so is to take the time to pay close attention to why the people in our lives are drawn to us, why they call us, and specifically what they like to talk to us about.

Most people have different kinds of people in their lives that they pick different kinds of fruit from or have different kinds of conversations with. Taking the time to conduct a personal survey to acknowledge what most people choose to talk to you about, or the kind of fruit that they pick from you, can be life changing. For many of us, the reasons others are drawn to us are consistent across the board. Some people are known to be the person who is called for a time of prayer or advice. Others are called when it's time to party.

Our responses to others have a great effect on the lives of the people around us. It's important for us to recognize that our words are fruit that people pick from us daily and, once consumed, create a reaction in their lives.

What's the Focus?

Take the time to assess who you have become
based on why people come to you.

Journal Questions:

* Why do most people come to you?

_____

_____

_____

_____

_____

_____

_____

_____

_____

_____

- What do people leave with after being with you?

_____

_____

_____

_____

_____

_____

_____

_____

_____

- What seeds has God planted in you for other people to eat from?

_____

_____

_____

_____

_____

_____

_____

_____

_____

Prayer: Dear heavenly Father, please help my words be the words that You want me to tell Your people as they come to me for direction and in general conversations. Let me not respond through my personal emotions but through Your exact direction. Let my voice be used to carry Yours.

7

Can God Add More to Your Life, or Are You "Just Working Here?"

Work hard so God can say to you, "Well done." Be a good workman, one who does not need to be ashamed when God examines your work. Know what His Word says and means.
—2 TIMOTHY 2:15 (TLB)

There are two types of employees: One goes to work, clocks in, does only what they're told to do, clocks out, and goes home. When asked a question about something other than what they may be working on at that particular moment, they shrug their shoulders and say, "I don't know. I'm just working here." They only work hard enough for the pay and benefits but never ask for more responsibility or show that they are capable of being used in any other way. They have no real interest in the company itself and would actually work for anyone who would pay them.

The other type of employee not only completes the tasks assigned but has a desire to learn more about the company they are working for, looks to build a relationship with the owner, and wants to gain a better understanding of their purpose there. They are grateful for having been chosen for the job and have faith that they will one day be promoted to do more.

Sometimes, when it comes to completing the jobs that God has assigned to us, we tend to act like we "just work here." We say to ourselves, "I'll do whatever God tells me to do, but then I'll keep moving on with my life," not realizing that the work that God has for us to do is supposed to *be* our lives.

We sometimes get so comfortable doing "small" assignments for God in an effort to complete our commitment but show no interest in committing to anything further. We have to do more than just clock in and out of what we understand to be God's work for our lives. Everything that happens in the natural comes from the spiritual, and just like when an employer sees that you are faithful, grateful, want to be used, are seeking a greater understanding of the company's ways, and want to build a relationship with the leadership, they will promote and use you more, so will God. We don't always look for the promotion that God has in store for us because it requires another level of growth and responsibility on our part. However, we must remind ourselves that working for the Lord is not only the most honorable job to have but is the only reason we were created.

What's the Focus?

Set a gold standard for the work that you do for God.

Journal Questions:

- Are you making yourself available for God to add more to your life?

_____

_____

_____

_____

_____

_____

_____

_____

_____

- In what areas can you increase your level of responsibility for the Lord?

_____

_____

_____

_____

_____

_____

_____

_____

_____

- In what areas of your life can you improve your time management to make more room for God's work?

_____

_____

_____

_____

_____

_____

_____

_____

_____

Prayer: Dear heavenly Father, please adjust my mindset to focus on my service to You. Help me to understand how capable I am through You and Your strength, direction, and favor. Help me to enjoy the opportunities You have created for me to serve You and Your people.

8

A Miracle Cannot Be Contained in a Box

Remember the wonders He has performed, His
miracles, and the rulings He has given.

—1 CHRONICLES 16:12 (NLT)

But as the Scriptures say, "No one has ever seen, no
one has ever heard, no one has ever imagined what
God has prepared for those who love Him."

—1 CORINTHIANS 2:9 (ERV)

People love to talk about the proper ways to travel on the road to success. They often speak as though there are only a few standard ways to get there. However, when God sets us up to be a part of a miracle, the miracle will never be standard, nor will it be able to be contained in a box with all the other things that people have done before.

When God tells us to do something and we seek the knowledge of other people *first*, we will often hear phrases like, "No one is going to look at what you have until you …," "It's not standard to do what you're doing," and "No one has done this before."

These sayings are red flags that we should be excited to hear. They remind us that God has ordered our steps and that He has a special path for our lives. A miracle cannot be compared to the standard practice because it is something that is amazing, phenomenal, unique, and out of the ordinary that only God can put into place.

What's the Focus?

Don't be distracted by ordinary requirements
on your way to becoming extraordinary.

Journal Questions:

•   What out-of-the-box miracle have you seen God do?

_____

_____

_____

_____

_____

_____

_____

_____

_____

_____

•   What extraordinary vision is God leading you to complete?

_____

_____

_____

_____

_____

_____

_____

_____

_____

- What unconventional direction are you struggling to pursue?

_____
_____
_____
_____
_____
_____
_____
_____
_____
_____

Prayer: Dear heavenly Father, please help me to understand that I am in the world but not of the world, and therefore I come to situations with Your unique direction that is not like those typical to this place. God, please help me to keep my ear focused on Your direction and not be swayed by others when You have given me a specific directive.

9

Don't Let Doubt Be a Tumor That Kills Your Faith

Jesus answered, "The truth is, if you have faith and no doubts, you will be able to do the same as I did to this tree. And you will be able to do more. You will be able to say to this mountain, 'Go, mountain, fall into the sea.' And if you have faith, it will happen. If you believe, you will get anything you ask for in prayer."
—MATTHEW 21:21–22 (ERV)

Sometimes when God gives us an idea along with a plan, our faith is the only thing that we have to hold onto as we move forward to complete the work.

However, if we do not trust God completely, even a tiny bit of doubt can act as a tumor that can destroy the plans. A cancerous tumor, although small, tends to spread fast and destroy everything that it touches. Sometimes due to circumstances that are related to the process, it becomes hard for us to continue to be able to clearly see the vision that was given to us or even believe that it was God's voice that we heard in the first place. When doubt begins to cover our faith and our faith is destroyed by doubt, we find ourselves stranded between our current situation and our intended destination. However, a healthy dose of faith will always wipe out doubt. We must be faithful, hold on, and trust God and His ways.

What's the Focus?

Don't let your lack of faith
destroy everything that you are working to build.

Journal Questions:

- What area of your life or assignment are you most uncertain of?

_____

_____

_____

_____

_____

_____

_____

_____

_____

- How can your disbelief destroy what you're working on?

_____

_____

_____

_____

_____

_____

_____

_____

_____

_____

- What is one thing that you can do every day to show God that you trust His process (e.g., communicating with Him through prayer and praise or committing to completing the action items He has provided for you)?

Prayer: Dear heavenly Father, please help me to increase my faith. Remind me, Lord, that You have always been in control and that when I trust in You and follow Your ways, I will be successful in all that You have set out for me to do.

10

Let This Scene Play Through

Let the Lord lead you and trust Him to help.
—PSALM 37: 5 (CEV)

I know the plans I have in mind for you, declares
the LORD; they are plans for peace, not disaster,
to give you a future filled with hope.
—JEREMIAH 29:11 (CEB)

Oftentimes we find ourselves in the middle of a scene in the movie of our lives and want so desperately to fast forward through it so that we can see what happens next, or we even have a desire to rewrite certain aspects of it. We want to make adjustments that we believe will work best for our overall story.

However, we must remember that we are only the actors in the scene; God has already written the script, and He is *the* director on set. We have no idea how our stories are supposed to end. We are supposed to read the scenes as they are delivered to us on a scene-by-scene basis.

God may reveal to us that certain things will happen, but we still have to follow His script all the way through so that we don't miss the pages that hold the lessons that we will need along the way. We sometimes get impatient about our circumstances and the things that are not happening in the "right now" of our lives. God's plan cannot always be seen but is often revealed on the next page.

We have to keep reading, trusting, and having faith while moving forward and relying on Him and His Word. We often make changes to His script based on our emotions and are then forced to sit back and wait for Him to rewrite our wrongdoing. It's imperative that we are patient and stay tuned to watch how God has already worked everything out on our behalf.

What's the Focus?

When God writes or rewrites the script of your life,
let the scenes play all the way through while following His direction.

Journal Questions:

- What are you on the verge of rewriting in the script of your life?

_____

_____

_____

_____

_____

_____

_____

_____

_____

_____

- How do you know that the changes in the direction of your next steps are aligned with God?

_____

_____

_____

_____

_____

_____

_____

_____

_____

- How can you ensure that you stay committed to the script that God has provided for your life?

_____

_____

_____

_____

_____

_____

_____

_____

Prayer: Dear heavenly Father, please help me have the patience to wait for You to reveal what You have for me to do next. Help me to pick up the lessons that You have packed into my journey along the way, and prepare me for the next scene that You have already written for my life.

11

Pay Attention to What
God Is Showing You

I have told you these things while I am still with
you. But the Holy Spirit will come and help you,
because the Father will send the Spirit to take my
place. The Spirit will teach you everything and will
remind you of what I said while I was with you.
—JOHN 14:25–26 (CEV)

Often as we walk down the road of life, God will take the time to carefully point out and explain to us things that are noteworthy along the way. He will guide us to and through certain places so that He can show us specific scenarios that are merely reflections of things to come.

Just as a parent walks a child through a garden explaining that although flowers may look and smell different, they are all still flowers, and although snakes come in difference sizes and colors, they are still snakes, God does this with us through our daily walk with Him. We must take the time to listen and get the most out of the situations that we are put into so that if we find ourselves there again, we will be able to say, "I know what this is because I have seen a version of this before. I will not be distracted by this again but will recognize it for what it is and push forward."

What's the Focus?

Pay attention to what God is showing you while you have the time.

Journal Questions:

- What are some things that you have ignored in the past that you wish you would have paid attention to?

_____

_____

_____

_____

_____

_____

_____

_____

_____

- What are some lessons that God has taught you along the way that you are still using for your benefit?

_____

_____

_____

_____

_____

_____

_____

_____

_____

- What is God showing in this part of your journey that is worth noting for future use?

_____

_____

_____

_____

_____

_____

_____

_____

_____

_____

Prayer: Dear heavenly Father, please show me in this season things that You want me to be aware of. Guide my focus so that I am attentive to all that You are trying to teach me. Please help me to understand the lessons that You are teaching me that can be duplicated for further use along my journey.

12

Surround Yourself with People Who Remind You to Have Great Posture

He who walks with wise men will be wise, but the
one who walks with fools will be destroyed.
—PROVERBS 13:20 (NLV)

Do not let anyone fool you. Bad people can make
those who want to live good become bad.
—1 CORINTHIANS 15:33 (NLV)

Having great posture generally comes from making a conscious effort to stand up straight even when it may not be the most comfortable position to be in.

For our spines, however, it is the best stance for us to take. Our spines were designed to support our weight and protect our spinal cords, the vital link from our brains to the rest of our bodies. It's much easier for us to slouch and slump over because it takes no effort. Because our spinal nerves affect all parts of our bodies, problems in our spines can cause other problems as well. However, if we make a habit of standing up straight, over time it will seem like the natural thing to do.

The same thing applies to our spirits. Our spirits support the weight in our lives (or our lives' challenges) and are the vital link between God and us. It is important that we make a conscious effort to stand up straight and create a habit of doing the right thing even when it may not be the most comfortable position to stand in. Because our spirits affect all parts of our lives, problems that occur with our spirits can cause other problems in our lives as well. People will often encourage us to slouch over like they do because, when we stand tall in our spiritual walk and they refuse to, they feel as though it makes them appear smaller. They will tell us that it's not natural to stand up straight all the time. Part of this is true because standing up straight by God's standards doesn't come from the natural but from the spiritual. When you surround yourself with people who are standing tall, they remind you to do the same through example.

What's the Focus?

Surround yourself with people who inspire you to grow, stand up taller and straighter and be better than you are today.

Journal Questions:

- In what areas of your life have you started to slouch or relax your standards?

- Who are the people in your life who allow you to slouch?

_____

_____

_____

_____

_____

_____

_____

_____

_____

- Who are the people who remind you to stand straighter?

_____

_____

_____

_____

_____

_____

_____

_____

_____

Prayer: Dear heavenly Father, please help me to stand tall on Your behalf. Please guide me to those whom You would have be great examples for me and my walk with You. Allow me to be drawn to great men and women who represent You and Your Word.

13

Allow God to Be Your Life's Preserver

When you go through deep waters and great troubles, I will
be with you. When you go through rivers of difficulty, you will
not drown! When you walk through the fire of oppression, you
will not be burned up—the flames will not consume you.
—ISAIAH 43:2 (NLT)

Anyone who calls upon the name of the Lord will be saved.
—ROMANS 10:13 (TLB)

Sometimes when we feel that we have been thrown into the deep
end of our lives and are drowning in troubles, we panic and become
extremely still or simply forget to breathe.

Although we understand that we are supposed to hand all our problems
over to the Lord, we often won't ask for help because of our shame,
embarrassment, guilt, and often pride. We try so hard and for so long
to save ourselves that we wait until we're almost drowning before we
ask for a life preserver to keep us afloat. God devised a technique that
has given us the ability to be saved from drowning in water; by merely
calming down, truly having faith, and believing that we will be okay,
we have the capability to float to the top of the water. However, if we
panic and move too fast, we will drown.

The same principles apply to the trying situations in our lives. If we
move too fast in our reactions or get wound up emotionally about our
issues rather than holding onto God as He carries us to safety, we can
drown. A lack of faith carries a lot of weight that will pull us down.

The word *float* also means "to glide," which means to move with a smooth, continuous motion. God can move us out of our situations smoothly if we allow Him to.

What's the Focus?

When life gets rough, *make* the time to calm down in the peace of the Lord so that you don't drown.

Journal Questions:

- What do you reach for when you feel like you're drowning?

_____

_____

_____

_____

_____

_____

_____

_____

_____

- How long do you normally wait before you ask for help?

_____

_____

_____

_____

_____

_____

_____

_____

_____

- How can you better communicate with God so that you don't get to a state of panic?

_____

_____

_____

_____

_____

_____

_____

_____

_____

Prayer: Dear heavenly Father, thank You for always being there for me. Thank You for saving me time and time again. I am so grateful that I can call upon You in phases of doubt and nervousness, knowing that You will preserve my life for good. Thank You, Father, for all that You do to make sure that I am taken care of.

14

Do Not Extend Contracts That God Has Not Signed Off On

God's way is perfect. All the Lord's promises prove true.
He is a shield for all who look to him for protection.
—PSALM 18:30 (ERV)

We are often quick to extend "contracts" to people in our lives without first going to God to gain confirmation on whether or not they are the right people we should be working or partnering with. We tend to rush into things before receiving God's "signature" of approval.

Whether it is within our businesses or personal relationships, we must allow God to show us what positions (if any) the people who come into our lives are to take. In business, a contract is not official without a proper signature from whoever is ultimately responsible and in charge of everything. Although we have been given the authority to manage our lives, it is important for us to understand that the final say, or confirmation, should always come from God.

Only He knows the full extent of what could happen within the deal that we are hoping to put into place. Every business deal that we make or personal relationship that we decide to get involved in should have His stamp of approval prior to our commitment. Our personal approval does not come with the same foresight or protection that God's does.

What's the Focus?

Always make sure that you are hearing from God
before you give approval for anything that is to happen in your life.

Journal Questions:

- What potential deals and or relationships do you have on the table
  right now that are waiting to receive God's approval?

_____

_____

_____

_____

_____

_____

_____

_____

_____

- What risks are associated with making the wrong decisions?

_____

_____

_____

_____

_____

_____

_____

_____

_____

_____

- What structure will you put into place in order to make sure you have God's approval before you make agreements with others?

_____
_____
_____
_____
_____
_____
_____
_____
_____
_____

Prayer: Dear heavenly Father, I thank You for allowing me the authority to make decisions surrounding the situations that You allow me to be placed in. I recognize, however, that everything that I authorize should be in alignment with Your will because my work is ultimately being carried out on Your behalf. Please prepare me to know when to give approval and when to decline on a deal, relationship, house, and so on. Please bless me with discernment to hear directly from You.

15

How Long Will You Praise Before You Complain?

I will answer them before they even call to me. While they are still talking about their needs, I will go ahead and answer their prayers!
—ISAIAH 65:24 (TLB)

The poor and needy search for water, but there is none; their tongues are parched with thirst. But I the LORD will answer them; I, the God of Israel, will not forsake them.
—ISAIAH 41:17(NIV)

When we go to God through prayer and ask Him to deliver all that we need, He will often send us a notice of confirmation letting us know that what we need is well on its way. Sometimes He will tell us directly how we should expect to receive what we're asking for. Other times He will send someone to us who is carrying a message that explains how the blessing will be delivered. For example, when we need a job, the confirmation may come in the form of an offer to interview for a new position. When we have a financial need, it may come from someone calling us to let us know that, for some unexpected reason, they will be sending a check to us in the mail.

When we first receive the notice of confirmation, we immediately begin to praise God, thanking and telling Him that we knew He could and would take care of our every need. In that moment we are able to see that He has answered our prayer request.

But at times when we are waiting for a couple of days or even a couple of weeks and we have yet to hear back about the job that we interviewed for or haven't received the check in hand, we start to complain even in the most subtle way. We'll say things like, "Lord, now, you said or you sent the confirmation that you were sending the money that I need, and you know that my deadline is coming up." Or we will say things like, "I haven't heard from the job that I interviewed for, Lord, and I thought that you set that interview up for me because you know that I need this job."

These are bold statements to God that let Him know that we are in doubt and questioning whether or not the confirmation came from Him. God is the One who sent the confirmation that His blessings and goodness were on their way in the first place and that He is our light out of our dark situation. Rather than continuously talking about our situation and complaining when we have not yet received what God said was on its way to us, we are to praise Him and give thanks until it arrives. The term "exercising your faith" implies that it is something that we have to continuously do in an effort to keep it strong.

What's the Focus?

Continue to praise God for the things that He has promised before and after you receive them.

Journal Questions:

- What are you waiting on God to do in your life, and what risks are associated with being impatient?

_____

_____

_____

_____

_____

_____

_____

_____

_____

_____

- How are you reacting to God and responding to others during your waiting process?

_____

_____

_____

_____

_____

_____

_____

_____

_____

_____

- How can you make sure that you're always in a state of praise?

_____
_____
_____
_____
_____
_____
_____
_____
_____
_____
_____

Prayer: Dear heavenly Father, please help me to stay focused on Your process. Help me to appreciate Your timing and trust that everything that you do happens in Your perfect timing. Please, Lord, help me to hear any words of complaint before they leave my mouth.

16

Do Not Let an Impulse Destroy God's Plans for Your Life

Don't be impatient for the Lord to act! Keep traveling steadily along His pathway and in due season He will honor you with every blessing, and you will see the wicked destroyed.
—PSALM 37:34 (TLB)

Bridle your anger, trash your wrath, cool your pipes—it only makes things worse.
—PSALM 37:8 (MSG)

Through our prayers, we often plant seeds into our lives that we want God to grow. Through our faith, we understand that if our plans are aligned with God's will, they will come to pass.

There are times, however, when we get frustrated because we haven't yet heard a word from God on when our seeds will grow into something that can be seen and felt. Even though the soil of our situation appears to be healthy *and* God is watering us with lessons on how we are to manage the harvest that is coming, we grow impatient.

It is important to remember that a seed grows quietly. You have to be completely tuned in to hear the confirmation of its crackling open. During these periods, we can get so discouraged about the timing of what we don't see happening in the soil that we let our impulses lead us to kick the dirt that our seeds have been planted into.

"Kicking the dirt" means talking about situations as though we've lost our hope or disregarding the plans that we have been working on for months because the process is taking much longer than we expected. When we kick the soil that is on top of our seed out of anger, we often kick the flowering bud of God's gift for our lives that was just about to pierce through the soil. We must pray and wait on God during those quiet times that He allows us to have with Him and spend our time asking, "What am I supposed to be learning right now that will make my situation better once you allow me to have what I have asked for?"

What's the Focus?

Don't accidentally destroy the gift
that God is preparing for you
based on your emotions.

Journal Questions:

- What situations have you prolonged or made worse through your emotional responses?

_____

_____

_____

_____

_____

_____

_____

_____

_____

_____

- When you're waiting on God to speak or deliver His promise, do you talk to Him about your emotions or do you talk to others about Him?

_____

_____

_____

_____

_____

_____

_____

_____

- What can you do while you wait on God that will help your process when you receive what He is sending to you?

_____

_____

_____

_____

_____

_____

_____

_____

Prayer: Dear heavenly Father, please help me with my patience while I wait on Your promises. Help me to remember that it was You who created the plans for my life, and it is You who will see me through to the end. Lord, I recognize that my impatience and emotional upset will only make things worse, but if I wait on You, You will honor me with every blessing.

17

How Can You Pass the Class If You Will Not Prepare for the Test?

After you have suffered a little while, our GOD who is full of kindness through Christ, will give you HIS eternal glory. He personally will come and pick you up, and set you firmly in place, and make you stronger than ever. To HIM be all the power over all things, forever and ever. Amen

—1 PETER 5:10–11 (TLB)

If you will humble yourself under the mighty hand of GOD, in HIS good time He will lift you up.

—1 PETER 5:6 (TLB)

Many of us so desperately want to pass a class or get through a challenge that we are facing. When beginning a trial, we often recognize that getting through it will release us into our next level. Even though we all want a great testimony, very few of us are excited to sign up for our test. Sometimes it just seems much easier to procrastinate on signing up for (or being willing to move toward) the final exam attached to the challenge rather than going through whatever is required and get past it.

In order to pass a test, we have to prepare for it. It's difficult, however, to prepare if we don't listen to our teacher, don't take notes during class, and refuse to look directly at our problems. Sometimes when students take classes like algebra, they feel like the class is a waste of time and cannot foresee how it could ever benefit their lives. We have to remember that when God tells us to do something, it is because He already understands our problems, has the right solutions, and knows how His instructions are relevant to our future.

We prepare for our tests by first taking a real look at the information that God has provided for us to see and experience, fully committing to doing the work at hand, studying our assignments, and paying close attention so that we will be promoted through our test to our testimony. A testimony is like a certificate that states, "I have made it through a learning experience of some sort by God's grace."

What's the Focus?

Every level of growth requires a level of testing.

Journal Questions:

- What areas of your life are you being tested in?

_____

_____

_____

_____

_____

_____

_____

_____

_____

_____

- When God presents a challenge, how do you prepare for it?

_____

_____

_____

_____

_____

_____

_____

_____

_____

- How will you better prepare for the challenges with which God presents you?

_____

_____

_____

_____

_____

_____

_____

_____

_____

Prayer: Dear heavenly Father, thank You for always being available to set me firmly in a place that you have created for me, regardless of what I am growing through. I thank You for thinking enough of me to challenge me to move into the next step of Your will and understanding. Thank You for making me stronger at every level through Your strength.

18

If We Put Ourselves in a Race with Everyone Else, We Will Have to Compete in Everyone Else's Race

Everyone should look at himself and see how he
does his own work. Then he can be happy in what
he has done. He should not compare himself with
his neighbor. Everyone must do his own work.
—GALATIANS 6:4–5 (NLV)

Don't copy the behavior and customs of this world but
be a new and different person with a fresh newness in
all you do and think. Then you will learn from your own
experience how HIS ways will really satisfy you.
—ROMANS 12:2 (TLB)

Recognizing that we are not in a race with anyone else in life can make it easier for us to both understand and run on the track that God has specifically prepared for us. If we allow God's will to be done and choose the route that He has designed for us, we won't have to worry about our next steps.

We are supposed to trust God, believing that our path has already been set with a destination full of great things to come. Obstacles will certainly appear, but we will have an easier time getting through them when we understand that they have been allowed for a purpose. For example, when looking for a job, home, or whatever the next challenge, it's important to recognize that the multiple interviews and searches are *simply* to build our faith, strength, and experiences. Sometimes, it is hard to understand that going through the process is for our benefit and that the process has been set in place to help us acquire the knowledge that we'll need once we reach our destinations and goals.

We cannot allow ourselves to give up when we don't get what we asked for or stress when someone else excels in a situation that is similar to ours. We have to stop and thank God for the experiences within the process. We must go through every door asking God to open our eyes and show us why we were sent there. Oftentimes, the purpose of the meetings that God sets up for us is different from what we initially anticipated. We have to ask God in every situation to give us what He has set aside for us. Who wants to compete with everyone else for something generic when God has already custom made something that specifically fits our personal needs and purpose? People who are the most successful are usually not competing with other people or using other people's common methods; instead, they typically rise to the top following the original paths that were created for them.

What's the Focus?

If you are not climbing the exact ladder that God created
for your life, you will never reach your true level of success.

Journal Questions:

- How do you measure your level of success?

_____

_____

_____

_____

_____

_____

_____

_____

_____

- How will you prevent yourself from being sidetracked by other people's races?

_____

_____

_____

_____

_____

_____

_____

_____

_____

- What is the finish line in the current leg of the race that you are running?

_____

_____

_____

_____

_____

_____

_____

_____

_____

Prayer: Dear heavenly Father, please remind me of my purpose at times when I am doubtful of the specific plan that You have designed for my life. Lord, please allow me to see the uniqueness of my path and the steps that I am to complete daily.

19

What Are You Sewing into Your Life?

Don't be misled: No one makes a fool of God. What a person
plants, he will harvest. The person who plants selfishness,
ignoring the needs of others—ignoring GOD!—harvests a crop
of weeds. All he'll have to show for his life is weeds! But the one
who plants in response to GOD, letting GOD's Spirit do the
growth work in him, harvests a crop of real life, eternal life.
—GALATIANS 6:7–9 (MSG)

Many of us are familiar with the phrases, "You reap what you sow"
and "You are what you eat." Both state that whatever we plant
into our lives will not only grow but ultimately affect a great part of
who we become.

If we plant poisonous fruits in our gardens and then eat them, our
bodies will become filled with poison. But if we sow seeds that add
the nutrients that we need, we will become stronger and our lives will
reflect health and strength.

Years ago, people would sew together blankets and fill them with
different materials based on their need to be covered and warm. The
materials were selected, placed into the fabric of the blankets, and
sown into what then became the blanket itself.

We make choices every day based on what we allow to be placed into
the fabric of our lives. What is placed in our lives ultimately becomes
our life stories. Every "yes" that we give others pertaining to our
journeys becomes another stitch that helps to cover our lives. We have

to decide what we want to cover us and then make sure that we are sowing those things into our lives.

What's the Focus?

The seeds you sew into your life are what will surround your steps.

Journal Questions:

- What seeds produced your current circumstances?

_____

_____

_____

_____

_____

_____

_____

_____

_____

_____

- What things have you sewn into your life that need to be uprooted?

_____

_____

_____

_____

_____

_____

_____

_____

_____

_____

_____

- What seeds will you intentionally sew moving forward?

_____

_____

_____

_____

_____

_____

_____

_____

_____

Prayer: Dear heavenly Father, please help me to be intentional about every seed that I sow. Let me not waste the seeds that You have provided me with but plant them carefully in great soil. Lord, please help me water and tend to the gifts that You have given me. Let me see what You have provided me with grow in a way that could only be predestined by You.

20

Do Not Put Artificial Plants on Top of Planted Seeds

But he finds joy in the Law of the Lord and thinks about His Law day and night. This man is like a tree planted by rivers of water, which gives its fruit at the right time and its leaf never dries up. Whatever he does will work out well for him. Sinful men are not like this. They are like straw blown away by the wind.

—PSALM 1:2–4 (NLV)

The Bible says that when we focus on God, we will be planted firmly like a tree and continuously blessed with leaves that do not die but prosper. However, if we go away from God, our leaves will blow away.

God has planted so many seeds into our lives by way of ideas and opportunities. Sometimes we get a bit frustrated when we feel that our seeds are not growing fast enough and may find it to be easier to replace them with artificial plants. The fact that the word *artificial* means "false," "fake," "imitation," and "man-made" reminds us that it can never really be a substitute for the real thing that God has designed for us. When we put artificial plants on top of planted seeds, neither will grow into what was meant for us to have or what we really need.

What's the Focus?

When you do what God wants you to do, you will be blessed,
but being impatient can ruin your opportunities.

Journal Questions:

- How quick are you to replace God's vision with your will?

_____

_____

_____

_____

_____

_____

_____

_____

_____

- How long does it typically take for you to develop a back-up plan
  in case God's plan takes longer than expected?

_____

_____

_____

_____

_____

_____

_____

_____

_____

_____

- Are you willing to go through the process of being deeply rooted in God's plan?

_____

_____

_____

_____

_____

_____

_____

_____

_____

Prayer: Dear heavenly Father, please teach me to be patient and follow Your instructions for my life so that I can be deeply rooted in Your will. Father, help me to see that there are no substitutes for Your plans and that You are the only one who can add true stability to my life.

21

Allow God to Set the Stage for Your Performance

Put GOD in charge of your work, then what
you've planned will take place.
—PROVERBS 16:3 (MSG)

Oftentimes when God gives us an assignment that we need to carry out or something that we need to state on His behalf, we get so excited by the big picture that we forget that the entire process is God's production *and* that He does not need us for every part of the plan.

Rather than try to figure out how everything should happen, we have to step back and allow God to set the stage for whatever He is preparing. Our challenge is to concentrate solely on the portion of the work that we have been assigned and lead in that particular area until we have been given further instruction. We often become so engaged in the entire process of the production that we don't take the proper time to study and prepare for our roles. Rather, we begin to focus on what time the production is set to start, where the stage will be located, who will set the lights, who will attend the show, and so on and so forth. It's important that we keep rehearsing for the parts that God has for us to do so that when He reveals that it is time for us to go on stage and He shines the light on the work that He has prepared us to deliver, we are ready.

We tend to tell God that we are waiting on Him just as children tell their parents that they are ready to go and waiting on them. Just as a parent has the ability to see other things that need to be done before it's time to leave, God will sometimes postpone what we think we're ready for until we are actually prepared to go. When we allow God to take control of our lives and accept the roles that He has for us, He will then invite the people He has chosen to be a part of what we were chosen to be a part of. He will also advertise our work and put everything else in order for His production.

What's the Focus?

Concentrate on the role that God has assigned to your life
rather than who and what is affiliated with it.

Journal Questions:

* What role has God assigned to you?

_____

_____

_____

_____

_____

_____

_____

_____

_____

_____

- What will it take for you to fulfill your role (e.g., learn your part, train, build)?

_____

_____

_____

_____

_____

_____

_____

_____

_____

_____

- How can you work to solely concentrate on your role?

_____

_____

_____

_____

_____

_____

_____

_____

_____

Prayer: Dear heavenly Father, I put You in charge of my work so that what You have planned for my life will take place. Lord, I recognize that you do not need me for every part of Your plan. I boldly accept my part and will patiently wait on Your execution.

22

Everyone Cannot Swim on Your Team

My dear friends, stand firm and don't be shaken.
Always keep busy working for the Lord. You know
that everything you do for HIM is worthwhile.
—1 CORINTHIANS 15:58 (CEV)

Iron is made sharp with iron, and one man is sharp by a friend.
—PROVERBS 27:17 (NLV)

Oftentimes after we discover our purposes, we become so excited that we want to bring everyone we know and love with us on our journeys to be a part of our teams.

However, we must understand that our purposes were not predestined for everyone else, nor was everyone else's purpose assigned to us. When God gives us something to do, we must allow Him to be the scout who brings our teammates to us based on His purpose for both our lives as well as theirs. Although we have been created to help as many people as we can and to be a blessing as we are being blessed, we must take the time to ask God how His people are to fit into the puzzle of our lives.

Some people are meant to work directly with us as we push forward on our day-to-day assignments. Others are there to cheer us on through our processes, celebrate with us after we have completed our tasks, and be blessed by our efforts. Through prayer and discernment, God will reveal the appropriate roles that have been set. God is the only scout who can determine who is truly best to "swim on our team." Only He truly knows who has the right qualifications to help fulfill the tasks that we have been given, who will make it to practice every day, who will be able to contribute special techniques, and who is able to hold still while underwater and only come up for air when necessary. People who swim in the shallow end of life are able to pop their heads out of the water more often because the water is not very deep. They do not always understand that when you are hard at work swimming in the deep end of life, you cannot come out of the water or take a break at any time to talk and socialize because you have to keep your focus. Although it is important to sit out by the pool and rest at times with our friends and loved ones, we must remember that once we're in the pool to swim, we should swim with people who were sent to us to be a part of our teams.

What's the Focus?

You don't get to choose who works with you on God's projects.
You do get to ask God to reveal His predetermined team.

Journal Questions:

- Do you consider God's will when bringing someone onto your team?

_____

_____

_____

_____

_____

_____

_____

_____

_____

_____

- How do you confirm whether that person has been assigned by God to work with you?

_____

_____

_____

_____

_____

_____

_____

_____

_____

- What steps will you take in the future to ensure that your top pick is God's top pick for the opportunity that you are looking to fill?

_____

_____

_____

_____

_____

_____

_____

_____

_____

Prayer: Dear heavenly Father, please align my work with those You have created to work with me. Help me to find those people who are not only passionate about the work that You have me doing but who are predestined and prequalified to add to it.

23

Are You Standing in the Middle of Your Miracle?

I will lead the blind on roads they have never known; I will guide them on paths they have never traveled. Their road is dark and rough, but I will give them light to keep them from stumbling. This is my solemn promise.
—ISAIAH 42:16 (CEV)

When God gives us a vision for a project or something that He wants us to do, His vision often creates an excitement within us that is like a paddle that pushes us into the middle of our purpose. Sometimes, however, once we're in the middle of the project, it's easy to feel tired, discouraged, and as though we're too far out into the ocean to turn back but not close enough to be on the other side. These are the times to remember the confirmation of the vision and that God will not take us anywhere that He will not bring us out of.

We have to keep pushing and paddling through to get to the other side. The exercise of paddling is what builds the strength and muscle (mentally and spiritually) that we will need in order to bear all that God has for us to manage and do through the process.

I once heard someone say that when we're going through and moving toward the vision that God has given us, we have to "keep our low beams on." He explained that when we're driving through darkness and don't know where we're going, God will flash His "high beam lights" so that we can see what's at the end of the road. He went on the say that it's our job to keep our low beams lights on while driving toward the vision so that we can pay close attention to every step of the road as we pass through. If we kept our high beam lights on, we would be distracted by the big picture and miss many lessons along the way.

What's the Focus?

Stay focused at every level. If you rush
through the middle of your process,
you will miss the lessons necessary for the end of your journey.

Journal Questions:

- Describe an experience that provided a lot of growth in the middle of the process, and tell what you learned along the way.

_____

_____

_____

_____

_____

_____

_____

_____

_____

- When your process or projects start to slow down, do you stop and pay attention to your surroundings or just try to figure out how to push forward at any cost?

_____

_____

_____

_____

_____

_____

_____

_____

_____

- In the future, how can you make sure that your process is noted along the way so that you can use what you have experienced for your upcoming journeys?

_____

_____

_____

_____

_____

_____

_____

_____

_____

Prayer: Dear heavenly Father, thank You for revealing certain things that You have set forth for my life's journey. Lord, as I step forward, please show me the lessons You have planted along the way for my growth that will help me when I get to where I'm going. Don't allow me to pass by lessons today that I will need to have experienced when I arrive tomorrow.

24

Never Fix a Vehicle That Has Been Totaled

You guide me with Your counsel, and
afterward You will take me into glory.
—PSALM 73:24 (NIV)

So don't remember what happened in earlier times. Don't
think about what happened a long time ago, because I
am doing something new! Now you will grow like a new
plant. Surely you know this is true. I will even make a road
in the desert, and rivers will flow through that dry land.
—ISAIAH 43:18–19 (ERV)

Insurance companies will not fix a vehicle that has been totaled. They understand that if a car has been destroyed and they make a minor fix to it, it will eventually still break down. They do not waste time, effort, or money on anything that will require more of an investment to fix it than it is actually worth in value.

We sometimes have a hard time because we don't stop to evaluate our situations and determine whether or not we are investing more into something than it is worth. It is important to recognize when something (e.g., relationships, people, jobs) has been damaged but is reparable versus when something has been destroyed or totaled.

Insurance companies would rather provide us with a new vehicle that will carry us to our destinations properly, although it may take us some time to adjust. God is our true insurance provider, and we have to learn how to stop wasting time, money, and effort on things in our lives that are broken that He refuses to fix. He will provide vehicles (or ways) to get us to where we need to go. However, when the vehicle or way that He has provided is no longer what He intends for us to use to continue on our journeys, He will warn us with signs. Things that have to do with our vehicles or ways will begin to break down. When He's ready, He will allow that vehicle to be totaled and will not fix it because it is no longer His will. He will, however, provide us with a new vehicle. Pay attention to your vehicle. Listen for signs. Pay attention to how it drives. Pray about it. Ask God to keep you safe as you go along your way. But if He wants you to let it go, be open to His new way.

What's the Focus?

Stop fixing things that are broken beyond repair.

Journal Questions:

- What relationship or situation have you tried to fix but is so broken that it simply never works properly?

_____

_____

_____

_____

_____

_____

_____

_____

_____

- In the past, what were the signs that something was beyond repair?

_____

_____

_____

_____

_____

_____

_____

_____

_____

- Are you willing to accept a new vehicle (e.g., relationship, job, situation) or are you insisting on keeping one that is broken because it is more comfortable? If so, why?

_____

_____

_____

_____

_____

_____

_____

_____

_____

_____

Prayer: Dear heavenly Father, please make it extremely clear when You are ready to replace something in my life. Help me to prepare for the new thing that You have for me and give me the ability to let go of things that are simply not working for the plans that You have for my life.

25

Are You Willing to Live in Fast-Forward?

The Lord, The Savior, The Holy One of Israel, says,
"I am The Lord your God. I teach you for your own
good. I lead you in the way you should go.
—ISAIAH 48:17 (ERV)

People frequently ask God, "When are *You* going to answer my prayers and move me into my next position in life?" God will move us to our next positions once we have mastered our current steps. In order to move past our current steps, we have to work through the experiences, lessons, and tests that have been built into each stride. God knows that different people move at different paces, and therefore the question is not "When are *You* going to move me, God?" but rather, "Am I willing to move forward at the same hurried pace that I am asking God to move in?"

God will not set us up to fail. He will not accelerate our lives unless we are willing to bear down and go through an accelerated process. He allows us to face tests and trials to make us wiser, stronger, and better prepared for our future. When a first-grade student is accelerated into the third grade, the school is not asserting that the child does not have to have the skills of a second grader but that the student has been tested for both the first and second grade and passed. They are conveying that the student has acquired the knowledge of both levels. In order to live in fast-forward, we have to be willing to study, test, and show ourselves approved for the success of the levels we're asking God to send us to.

What's the Focus?

Only ask God to move you forward
if you're willing to do what it takes to get there.

Journal Questions:

- What area of your life would you like God to accelerate your steps in (into a marriage, new job, new business, retirement, etc.)?

_____

_____

_____

_____

_____

_____

_____

_____

- What will you be required to do or know in order to be successful in the position you would like God to move you into?

_____

_____

_____

_____

_____

_____

_____

_____

- What are you willing to do and when are you willing to start preparing for what you're praying for?

_____

_____

_____

_____

_____

_____

_____

_____

_____

_____

Prayer: Dear heavenly Father, please show me what I can start doing right now in an effort to prepare for where You are taking me. I know that I want what You want for my life. I want to do more for You but also want to be prepared and ready so that You will be happy with my work.

26

Are You Ready to Get Picked Up?

Be dressed ready for service and keep your lamps
burning, like servants waiting for their master to return
from a wedding banquet, so that when he comes and
knocks they can immediately open the door for him.
—LUKE 12:35–36 (NIV)

Because Noah had faith, he built a large boat for his family. God
told him what was going to happen. His faith made him hear God
speak and he obeyed. His family was saved from death because
he built the boat. In this way, Noah showed the world how sinful
it was. Noah became right with God because of his faith in God.
—HEBREWS 11:7 (NLV)

God has made us what we are. In Christ Jesus, God made
us new people so that we would spend our lives doing
the good things he had already planned for us to do.
—EPHESIANS 2:10 (ERV)

We often state that we are ready to work with investors, agents, or employers and are waiting on God to take the vision that He has given us to the next level. The question that we have to ask ourselves is, "Am I really ready to get picked up?" If God sent someone to us right now to take our ideas or bodies of work to the market or hire us for the jobs that we say that we are standing by for, would we really be prepared? Are we able to explain our vision? Is our work packaged and ready to go?

God will often send "drivers" to us, people whom He has ordained to carry our work from one stage to the next. These drivers will come at God's appointed time to pick us up and take our work to the market. When factory workers produce a product, they do not worry about who is coming to pick it up. They understand that the owner of the company has already hired a driver to take it to the market. They do not worry about how it will be advertised because they understand that the owner has already hired a marketing and advertising company. What they focus on is the quality of their work and the timeline that has been set to complete it.

What's the Focus?

Get your work completely finished for God
to have it picked up and taken to the market.

Journal Questions:

- What projects or professional positions would you love for God to send someone to help you with right now?

_____

_____

_____

_____

_____

_____

_____

_____

_____

_____

- Are you 100 percent ready to be taken out to the market?

_____

_____

_____

_____

_____

_____

_____

_____

_____

- What can you do to be better prepared when He sends His representative to you?

_____

_____

_____

_____

_____

_____

_____

_____

_____

Prayer: Dear heavenly Father, please help me to personally prepare for my next steps ahead. Help me to see what I need to do in order to be 100 percent ready. Help me to package what I have prepared so that when You send Your people to take me to the market I will be ready. Please show me what I am missing and what I need to do so that time is not wasted when You are ready for me to move forward.

27

God's Will versus Free "Wheel"

So, I beg you, brothers and sisters, because of the great
mercy God has shown us, offer your lives as a living
sacrifice to him—an offering that is only for God and
pleasing to HIM. Considering what he has done, it is
only right that you should worship him in this way.
—ROMANS 12:1 (ERV)

Although God has shown us that He has a perfect will, or plan set for our lives according to His purpose, we still have to make the decision to have Him as our driving force. Being given the choice to have free will and live our lives as we please is like being able to drive ourselves into our own destiny. Children often express that once they're allowed to get behind the wheel and drive, they plan to go places and experience things that they have never experienced before.

Our understanding of having free will is often much like a child's. We get excited about being able to go off of the path that has been planned for us simply because we can. Like a child, we want to drive to places that we think will be great to explore. However, after driving on our own for so long in the wrong direction and being involved in accidents simply because we were in the wrong places, we often realize that it is so much easier to sit back and drive on the course that God has designed for us.

What's the Focus?

Just because you *can* go somewhere doesn't mean you should.

Journal Questions:

- When have you felt like you were in conflict with God's will for your life?

_____

_____

_____

_____

_____

_____

_____

_____

_____

- How do you gauge when you are off track with God's direction?

_____

_____

_____

_____

_____

_____

_____

_____

_____

_____

- How do you drive yourself back towards God's will when you find yourself going off track?

_____

_____

_____

_____

_____

_____

_____

_____

_____

Prayer: Dear heavenly Father, please help me to align my will with Yours. Stop me from getting so excited about moving toward things and people who are not approved by You for my life. Help me to be wise and only do things that are pleasing to You.

28

Where Is Your Route (or Life) Leading Others?

Don't be like a ruler over those you are responsible for. But be good examples to them.
—1 PETER 5:3 (ERV)

Within our daily lives, be it through our jobs in customer service, teaching, managing others, parenting, or even interactions with people whom we pass by on the street, the reflection of who we are should ultimately reflect the work that God has done within us. This reflection is what will often bring people to want to know God and have a personal relationship with Him as well.

Our lives are to be like buses whose destination is God while picking up other people along the way. We are not to be judgmental toward whomever we pick up but understand that some people will get onto our bus to get to know who God is while others know who He is but get on, or sit next to us, in an effort to get in tune with His direction for their lives. When it's time for the people on our bus to exit, or move out of our lives, it is not our place to question their actions but to understand that they are moving onward on their own routes. We must be willing to do God's will and remember that He will place us in areas and use us through our work to bring people closer to Him.

What's the Focus?

Who you are should make people want to be closer to God.

Journal Questions:

- When people get on your bus (or are around you), do they know that you are powered by God?

_____

_____

_____

_____

_____

_____

_____

_____

_____

- What would you like to incorporate into your day to help lead others to Christianity?

_____

_____

_____

_____

_____

_____

_____

_____

_____

_____

- What should you stop doing that is not a great reflection of being a child of God?

_____

_____

_____

_____

_____

_____

_____

_____

_____

_____

Prayer: Dear heavenly Father, please lead me in my daily walk to be a great reflection of who You are. Help me to be an amazing example who brings people to want to have a direct relationship with You after getting to know me. Enhance those things that You have used to draw people to me so that I can draw more people to You. Help my life's journey be one that is beneficial to others as they seek to have a greater relationship with You.

29

Are Your Words Driving You in the Wrong Direction?

Let no unwholesome word proceed from your mouth, but only such a word as is good for edification according to the need of the moment, so that it will give grace to those who hear.
—EPHESIANS 4:29 (NASB)

I tell you that everyone will have to answer for all the careless things they have said. This will happen on the Day of Judgment.
—MATTHEW 12:36 (ERV)

We usually have the best intentions when planning a trip toward the "right direction" of life. We clear our minds, pack our bags, and determine that we are going to make it to the right place.

When driving ahead, our intentions are like the body of a car, but our words are the tires that take us on our way. God tells us in the book of Mark that the words that we say, backed by faith, are so powerful that they can move mountains. He also said that we will have those things that we speak about out loud. We are reminded in Ephesians not to let any words come out of our mouths that are not a good lesson to those around us who are learning from our example.

For some reason, even when speaking about the great works that God has done in our lives, we still use words that roll us backward instead of in the right direction. Think about how many times you have heard someone say, "It is just so *crazy* what God is doing in my life" or "I have received so many blessings in my life that it is just *ridiculous.*" The word *crazy* means "foolish," "unwise," "idiotic," "senseless," and "weird." The definition of *ridiculous* is "without reason," "absurd," "ludicrous," and "meaningless." Although we may be rolling forward through our praise, the words that we use can cause us to roll backward. It is important to be mindful of the words that come out of our mouths as we continue on our journeys.

What's the Focus?

Your words can take you into places
that you have no intention of going.

Journal Questions:

- What words do you use that are not aligned with God's greatness for your life?

_____

_____

_____

_____

_____

_____

_____

_____

_____

_____

- How would you describe what God has done in your life?

_____

_____

_____

_____

_____

_____

_____

_____

_____

- How can you become more intentional about the words that you use?

_____

_____

_____

_____

_____

_____

_____

_____

_____

Prayer: Dear heavenly Father, please help me to watch my words. Help me to hear the words that are not like You before they leave my mouth and replace them with those that will reflect Your goodness.

30

Do Not Be Discouraged by the Size of Your Seed

Here is another of HIS illustrations: "The Kingdom of Heaven is like a tiny mustard seed planted in a field. It is the smallest of all seeds but becomes the largest of plants and grows into a tree where birds can come and find shelter."
—MATTHEW 13:31–32 (TLB)

Many of us are working hard to plant the seeds that God has given to us. We often try not to lose sight of His instructions in spite of the fact that the seed, or what He has given us to plant, may seem relatively small in comparison to what we have been told it will grow into.

It's important to remember that a seed is *always* substantially smaller than the plant it becomes. It is also important to understand that, in spite of its size, everything a seed will ever grow into is inside of it before it's planted. All of a tree's roots and branches and every piece of fruit that it is ever going to be borne is in the seed. The only thing it needs to grow is God's water and sunlight.

This is an example to us that, before God gives us our assignment or seed to plant in the world, He has already packed it with everything it will need to grow except for what He will use to water it along the way. We should not focus on whether it will grow but rather who will benefit from it and what God will have us do with the overflow.

What's the Focus?

When God gives you something that seems small,
get prepared for Him to multiply it according to His will.

Journal Questions:

- What seeds has God given you to plant (i.e., what vision have you
  been led to develop)?

_____

_____

_____

_____

_____

_____

_____

_____

_____

- Have you ever slowed down a process or stopped moving forward
  on completing a project because you felt as though you didn't have
  enough to complete what you initially envisioned?

_____

_____

_____

_____

_____

_____

_____

_____

_____

- What can you do in your day-to-day walk that can help you to remember that God will always give you what you need in order to finish the work He led you to begin (e.g., pray, write the vision out as a reminder, write down what He has already provided for the project, etc.)?

_____

_____

_____

_____

_____

_____

_____

_____

_____

Prayer: Dear heavenly Father, I thank You, Lord, for blessing me with a seed to plant. Thank You for sharing Your ideas with me and allowing me to work on Your plan to carry them out. I trust that whatever You have given to me is more than enough for me to get Your work started and that You will water and grow it as You see fit.

31

Allow Yourself to Be Deeply Rooted

But they who wait upon the Lord will get new strength.
They will rise up with wings like eagles. They will run and
not get tired. They will walk and not become weak.
—ISAIAH 40:31 (NLV)

God is the one who enables you both to want
and to actually live out His good purposes.
—PHILIPPIANS 2:13 (CEB)

Are there times when you don't feel like going through a process even though you know it will lead you to your destination? Have you ever wanted God to literally plant you in the position that you'd like to be in?

For many of us, there are times when we want to be promoted without being planted. We'd like to be secured and grounded into our positions without having to take the time to grow roots. Although it's exciting to think about growing, it is also easy to become impatient with the time it can take to go from being a planted seed to a full-grown tree. God could easily plant us into the positions that we want to be in. But if He did, just like a tree that is placed on the sidewalk without being deeply rooted, after the rain or troubles came to pass, we could be swept away.

It's a tree's roots that carry what it needs to support its growth and keep it grounded. Many of us have asked God to plant us into our situations as the full version of the tree that we hope to be. However, it is important that we wait and allow the seed that God has planted in us to be deeply rooted by Him so that our purposes will be absorbed and filled with all that is required for it to serve God's purpose.

What's the Focus?

Don't rush the process that God is using to give you
the strength and knowledge that you're
going to need where you are going.

Journal Questions:

• Have you ever rushed through a process and realized you missed something along the way? If so, what did you miss?

_____

_____

_____

_____

_____

_____

_____

_____

_____

- What are you currently being deeply rooted into?

_____
_____
_____
_____
_____
_____
_____
_____
_____

- What are you praying for, along with God's strength that you know you will need in your new position?

_____
_____
_____
_____
_____
_____
_____
_____

Prayer: Dear heavenly Father, thank you for loving me so much that You would take Your time to make sure that I am prepared for where You are taking me. Please help me to remember as I wait patiently on You that You always have a plan tied to a timeline according to Your will.

32

It's Impossible to Shop in the Devil's Store and Come Out with God's Will

Why do you keep on saying that I am your
Lord, when you refuse to do what I say?
—LUKE 6:46 (CEV)

No servant can serve two masters; for either he will hate the
one and love the other, or else he will be loyal to the one and
despise the other. You cannot serve God and mammon.
—LUKE 16:13 (ESV)

We cannot take the customs of the world that we like, put a spin on them in our minds, and then think that we can justify our actions by saying, "Oh, I don't do this for that reason. I do it because …" We've been warned very specifically about certain things that we are not to partake in. It is not always easy, but we either do right by God's instructions or we do wrong and eventually suffer the consequences.

We often wonder why the devil will not leave us alone and why at times it seems that we cannot shake him. One of the reasons this happens is because there are certain things that we do to invite him into our lives. He's merely looking for a ride into our space, and we often create a ticket with his name on it by what we do, say, watch on television, and listen to on the radio.

In the Ten Commandments, we are told not to worship any other gods, which means we have an obligation to research the things that we keep close to us. We may, for example, want to purchase a piece of artwork because it's pretty, but if that piece of art is deemed to be a god somewhere else and worshipped, we have to consider whether it is something that we really want in our homes.

Some of us live by certain exercise classes that are popular for calming us down and keeping our bodies lean. But if the rituals surrounding specific exercise regimens are considered to be praise positions to other gods in other cultures, what goals are we accomplishing?

Things that we accept and rationalize in our minds today, God already knew would come to us in a pretty package. The question we have to answer for ourselves is, "Is the justification that we give ourselves today going to be enough of a justification to give to God later?"

What's the Focus?

If you're not following God when you are *not* doing
what He says, who are you following?

Journal Questions:

- What are two things that are deemed normal in society that are not aligned with God's directions?

_____

_____

_____

_____

_____

_____

_____

_____

_____

_____

- What have you done that is not aligned with God's Word that you regretted after the fact?

_____

_____

_____

_____

_____

_____

_____

_____

- How do you balance living in the world but not being of the world (i.e., being a child of God in a world that doesn't honor all His instructions)?

_____

_____

_____

_____

_____

_____

_____

_____

Prayer: Dear heavenly Father, please help me to recognize those things in this society that are not like You. Help me to disassociate with them simply because my desire is to associate with You. I recognize that I do not have to understand Your directions to follow them. I thank You, God, for being such an amazing Father who leads me along my way.

33

Are You Looking Both Ways When You Come to a Stop Sign?

Listen and hear my voice. Listen and hear my words.
—ISAIAH 28:23 (NLV)

My sheep recognize my voice, and I know
them, and they follow me.
—JOHN 10:27 (TLB)

As we're driving along in life, moving toward our next steps, we come to what seem to be stop signs along the way. Just as we do with stop signs on the street, it is important that in life we take a few moments to stop and look both ways before moving forward. When God brings us to a stop, it is a stop in our *process*, not our *progress*.

We are to look to the right and pay attention to the things that God is showing us while listening to what He is telling us about the drive ahead. We must pay closer attention to the people that He is sending to us and the conversations that they bring. Although we may not understand the significance of their words at the time, it is important that we remember to put their words in our pockets because they are often the keys that we will need to unlock issues in the future.

We must also look to the left and tune in to words that God may have for us to stop and share with others based on our prior experience. Many of us remember that the television show *The Amazing Race* was a huge success. The contestants who won were those who followed the first set of directions that were given to them most efficiently, which led them to their next steps and ultimately to their goal.

They were never given all the answers in advance. They learned to listen to those who were sent to give them the next bit of information that they needed. This forced them to pay close attention to the clues around them. Without question, they had faith that their clues would lead them to their final destination. That is how we are supposed to react to the clues that God sends to us. We need to follow His direction, looking closer at our situations without question, knowing that He will lead us to our final destination.

What's the Focus?

Pay closer attention to the reasons
behind the people and circumstances in your life.

Journal Questions:

- How often do you question why people are in your life or why you are going through something in particular?

_____

_____

_____

_____

_____

_____

_____

_____

_____

_____

- What have the closest three people in your past taught you?

_____

_____

_____

_____

_____

_____

_____

_____

_____

- What have you brought into the lives of the last three people you met?

_____

_____

_____

_____

_____

_____

_____

_____

_____

Prayer: Dear heavenly Father, help me to live on purpose. Show me what I am supposed to gain from the circumstances and people that You send into my life. Help me to know what I am supposed to share with others along the way. Help me to hear Your voice more clearly every day.

34

Be Prepared to Sharpen Your Pencil

Dear friends, don't be surprised or shocked that
you are going through testing that is like walking
through fire. Be glad for the chance to suffer as
Christ suffered. It will prepare you for even greater
happiness when He makes His glorious return. Count
it a blessing when you suffer for being a Christian.
This shows that God's glorious Spirit is with you.
—1 PETER 4:12–14 (CEV)

We should continue to sharpen our pencils (or prepare for our purposes) and remember that our handwriting (or work) is not its best when we are writing with dull lead.

Many companies require that their employees go through rigorous training and test them on their knowledge and ability to complete tasks. Companies make sure that employees are prepared for the job at hand before they are sent out to do work on their behalf.

God has given all of us jobs that we are to oversee or accomplish. Some require that we have the knowledge that would be equivalent to a high school diploma and others a bachelor's degree. Some positions require that we have an understanding at the level of a PhD.

We often get excited and accept positions before we realize how challenging they will be and that there will be tests that we'll have to pass in order to officially be qualified to do the work. Seeing what it may take to push through the process at times makes us want to give up, but we must understand that we cannot excel if we are not prepared.

A pencil is at its best after it has been pulled across sharp edges. We are to use the sharp edges of every challenge that we go through to sharpen our pencils and prepare for what's next. Once we have been sharpened, we will be able to be used for the task at hand. However, we must also remember that we will eventually need to be sharpened again. At that time, God will begin to prepare or make us sharper for the next job that will require that we go through yet another process.

What's the Focus?

Be grateful for the process God uses
to prepare you for the success of your life.

Journal Questions:

* What situations in your past has God had to sharpen or prepare you for?

_____

_____

_____

_____

_____

_____

_____

_____

_____

_____

- What did He use to sharpen or prepare you for greatness (e.g. a situation within your family or on your job, a financial hardship, a problem in your relationship)?

_____

_____

_____

_____

_____

_____

_____

_____

_____

- What should you tell yourself or how should you prepare yourself when you see trials or sharp edges coming your way?

_____

_____

_____

_____

_____

_____

_____

_____

_____

_____

Prayer: Dear heavenly Father, thank You for taking the time to prepare me for all that You have created for me to accomplish. I am so grateful to have such an amazing Father who looks at my steps ahead and designs my daily steps so that I am successful. I pray that You give me the wisdom to know when You are merely sending challenges my way to make me stronger and better for the journey that You have created for my life. I pray that I am able to trust with joy and faith as I move ahead.

35

What Are You Claiming in God's Name?

Moses answered, "I will tell the people of Israel that the
God their ancestors worshiped has sent me to them. But
what should I say, if they ask me your name?" God said to
Moses: I am the eternal God. So, tell them that the Lord
whose name is "I Am," has sent you. This is my name forever,
and it is the name that people must use from now on.
—EXODUS 3:13–15 (CEV)

Words can bring death or life! Talk too much,
and you will eat everything you say.
—PROVERBS 18:21 (CEV)

One of the names by which we know God as in the Bible is the
Great I Am. The book of John and the burning bush episode in
Exodus give examples of who the Great I Am is.

When Moses realized what the Lord was calling him to do, he began
to ask for confirmation for himself and for the children of Israel. In
reply to Moses's question, "Suppose ... they ask me, 'What is his name?'
Then what shall I tell them?" God responds by saying, "I am who I am."

When we think about the fact that God is the Great I Am and that
when we go before Him and pray we ask for everything in His name,
we should then consider how we use the words "I am" and the power
that they carry.

When we speak the words "I am," we are essentially claiming whatever we say after His name. When you say, "I am broke or broken," you are claiming that you are and will be broken. Be careful what you claim in God's name.

What's the Focus?

Be careful about what you are praying
into your life built on your daily words.

Journal Questions:

- What are your three most frequently used "I am" statements that you personally use about yourself daily (e.g., I am tired, I am excited, I am grateful)?

_____

_____

_____

_____

_____

_____

_____

_____

_____

_____

- How do you see your "I am" statements reflected in your life? Do you notice that what you state becomes your state of being?

_____

_____

_____

_____

_____

_____

_____

_____

_____

- What three "I am" statements will you intentionally sow into your life starting today?

_____

_____

_____

_____

_____

_____

_____

_____

_____

Prayer: Dear heavenly Father, thank you for being the Great I Am. Thank You for being so incredibly powerful that Your name alone makes changes to the earth and to the lives of Your people. God, please help me to remember that what I state becomes my state of being and that I am Your child and gifted with the privilege of using Your name to make changes in my life and in the lives of others. Please help me focus on my words and their meaning daily.

36

Do Not Delay Your Delivery

I am sure that what we are suffering now cannot
compare with the glory that will be shown
to us. In fact, all creation is eagerly waiting
for God to show who his children are.
—ROMANS 8:18–19 (CEV)

Some women have said that they would love to have a baby but do not want to physically "have a baby" because the thought of what they would have to go through to give birth seems overpowering. Mothers sometimes become overwhelmed when they initially find out that they are expecting a child. In the beginning it can seem a bit surreal, but at some point they are forced to face the fact that there is a person full of purpose growing inside of them. A lot of women embrace the stages that they go through and the beauty of the process. However, once the hard labor and contractions begin, some become so overwhelmed by the pain that they start to feel as though they want to give up. Regardless of how they respond to the pain, in order for the baby to live in its purpose, it has to be delivered.

The same thing often occurs when people find out that God has impregnated them with a very specific purpose that they are to give birth to and that it too will grow just as a baby grows inside of its mother's womb. Women are reminded that their babies are soon to come as they watch their bodies grow, develop, and change. God will send confirmation to us as well that our purposes are growing as we watch Him change and redevelop specific things in our lives in preparation for the birth of our purposes.

We, too, in many cases begin to embrace our purposes and the stages that they bring. We become excited to build on the visions that God has given to us. However, right before it is time to push out or deliver our purposes, the "pregnancy pains" that we are faced with oftentimes overwhelm us. We can either bear down and recognize that our purposes will be born and grow into what God has for them to be, or we can wait, turn our backs to the pain and discomfort, and decide that we are not ready to go through the labor pains that we are experiencing. If we push, the baby will be delivered. If we choose not to push, God may choose to use an extreme delivery method, or it may die within us. We have to remember that in all things, God works for the good of those who love Him who have been called according to His purpose.

What's the Focus?

Don't let the challenges that are tied to the delivery of your blessings delay your ability to receive what God has created for you.

Journal Questions:

- What has God birthed inside of you that you can feel His nudge to grow?

_____

_____

_____

_____

_____

_____

_____

_____

_____

_____

- What most excites you about it?

_____

_____

_____

_____

_____

_____

_____

_____

_____

_____

- What can you do to prepare yourself for the birth of your purpose?

_____

_____

_____

_____

_____

_____

_____

_____

_____

Prayer: Dear heavenly Father, thank You for blessing me with a purpose-filled assignment to add to Your kingdom. Thank You for Your patience as I grow to understand my assignment and for Your direction as I enter into it fully. Please give me the strength to push through when times are challenging, never forgetting that You never start something that You do not complete.

37

God Does Not Need Us for Every Part of the Plan

I know all the birds in the mountains, and every wild creature is in my care. If I were hungry, I wouldn't tell you, because I own the world and everything in it. I am God Most High! The only sacrifice I want is for you to be thankful and to keep your word.
—PSALM 50:11–12, 14 (CEV)

When we ask God to go before us and plan out or order our steps, He will begin to show us what He has already created for us to do in His will. He will give us direction and guide our footsteps along the way. As this begins to happen and we see things move in our favor, we usually feel motivated. However, when it seems as though our steps are slowing down, we tend to get anxious and feel nervous, wondering if the plans that God has shown us are at a standstill or have completely stopped.

We must remember that we are to do all that we are led to do and that God will do the rest. One songwriter tells us to stand still and wait on the Lord after we have done all that we can do. This is to remind us that we are a *part* of God's plan.

We are to listen, be obedient, follow His direction, and understand that we are not needed for every part of His plan, and that includes those plans that pertain to our own lives. There is absolutely no need for us to stress about situations after we have prayed about them and have followed His directions. God will not only go before us and order our steps, but after we leave the places that we have been sent to, He will continue to stay there and work things out on our behalf. During the quiet times when we start to think that nothing is happening, we are to continue to give Him praise and give thanks for the things that He *is* doing. We must show Him that although we don't see everything that He has done, we have faith, trust, and believe that He is in full control. Remembering that we are a part of His plan helps us to be patient during those quiet, still moments.

What's the Focus?

Stop worrying about the parts of the process
that you were not assigned to
and have more trust in God to complete His work.

Journal Questions:

* What parts of your process are you most concerned about because you have no control over them?

_____

_____

_____

_____

_____

_____

_____

_____

_____

_____

- How can you build your trust in God daily to help keep your nerves calm while you wait on His next move?

_____

_____

_____

_____

_____

_____

_____

_____

_____

- Are there parts of the plan over which you do have control that you have not completed? If so, what are they and how can you move them forward?

_____

_____

_____

_____

_____

_____

_____

_____

_____

Prayer: Dear heavenly Father, thank You for only giving me a part of Your plan to carry out. I am so grateful that You are so gracious and merciful that You would allow me to be a part of Your process but yet not overload me with more than I can bear to manage. Please help me to understand how important my portion of the work is to You.

38

What Are You Putting into Your Pockets?

The Lord says, "I will guide you along the best pathway
for your life. I will advise you and watch over you."
—PSALM 32:8 (NLT)

What are you picking up and putting into your pockets as you travel along the road of your life's journey? Everywhere we go, there are things (big and small) that we are supposed to pay attention to or put into our pockets as we move forward. These are the things and ideas that we are exposed to that at some point we will need to pull out or remember as we go along our way.

Periodically, we ignore what's going on around us when we feel as though it has nothing to do with our lives and that there is nothing that we can gain from paying attention to it. However, there are times when God will have us pick something up so that we can share it with someone else later for their benefit.

Have you ever given a testimony to someone about something that you experienced in the past that related exactly to what they were going through in the present? It may not be until such a moment that you stop to question whether or not God used you to go through your experience simply because He knew that He could then use you to help that person get through his or her experience. As we give and use the knowledge that we gain, if we listen and are attentive, God will continue to give us what we need as we move forward.

What's the Focus?

Don't discount what you're being exposed to
because, on God's path, everything is for purpose.

Journal Questions:

- How do you discern or determine what you give your attention to?

_____

_____

_____

_____

_____

_____

_____

_____

_____

- How often do you share relatable testimonies for the purpose of helping someone else?

_____

_____

_____

_____

_____

_____

_____

_____

_____

_____

- How intentional are you about taking mental notes on what you've experienced in your past so that they can help you reflect on your situations in the future?

_____

_____

_____

_____

_____

_____

_____

_____

_____

_____

Prayer: Dear heavenly Father, please help me to be more intentional about paying attention to what You are laying out in front of me for my growth. Please remind me when necessary that everything that I have been through is not just for me but that my testimony of my experiences can help expedite the shifting of the lives of others.

39

Check Your Oxygen Level

He doesn't need help from anyone. He gives life,
breath, and everything else to all people.
—ACTS 17:25 (CEV)

Oxygen is what we breathe in daily and need in order to live. Every time we inhale, it is carried to our cells and travels to our heart, which then pumps the oxygen-rich blood through our bodies. This gives us the energy that we need to function and move forward. Oftentimes when people have a hard time breathing, doctors will put them on a machine to make sure that they receive an adequate amount of oxygen.

Just as our bodies need oxygen, our spirits function in a similar way. However, God is the oxygen that makes our spirits function properly. When we take the time to praise and worship, we are breathing Him into our spirits. We must check our breathing constantly, deeply inhaling His presence. He also touches our hearts, giving us the energy needed to function and move forward in His will. It is important that we are mindful of what we allow ourselves to breathe in. Neither our bodies nor our spirits were designed to function at their best when covered in pollution.

When our spiritual breathing gets rough, it is important that we pray and ask God to give us a direct infusion of Him. Breathing works two ways: in and out. When we breathe God in, what we breathe out onto others is greatly affected.

What's the Focus?

Allow God to be the air you breathe
throughout the day that sets your atmosphere.

Journal Questions:

- Do you start your morning breathing God into your day or suffocating in the pollution around you?

_____

_____

_____

_____

_____

_____

_____

_____

_____

_____

- How do you clear the air around you?

_____

_____

_____

_____

_____

_____

_____

_____

_____

_____

- When the air around you gets thick, do you put your "oxygen mask" on first (or check in with God through prayer) before attempting to help those around you?

_____

_____

_____

_____

_____

_____

_____

_____

_____

_____

Prayer: Dear heavenly Father, please breathe and add inspiration into my life throughout the day so that my spirit, heart, and mind will function at the level that pleases You. Help me to recognize when the air around me is thick, cloudy, and not like You so that I can work to move into a healthier space that You would have me to be in.

40

Be Careful about Taking Directions from Someone Who Has Not Been Where You're Going

May the Lord send help from His temple and
come to your rescue from Mount Zion.
—PSALM 20:2 (CEV)

Before asking for directions or advice for your life, do you make it a habit to find out if the person you are asking is qualified to give you the correct information? When asking for driving directions, the most common questions that are asked first are, "Do you live around here?" and "Are you familiar with this area?"

We don't always take those questions into consideration when trying to determine what our next steps in life should be. We sometimes feel more comfortable talking to a friend about our situation rather than speaking with someone we don't know, even though they may be more familiar with what we're going through and have actually been sent to help us get through our situation.

When we are serious about seeking the knowledge that we need in order to move forward, we must first seek directions from God, asking Him to place us with people who are qualified to help us get through what we're experiencing and can help direct us to where we need to go.

What's the Focus?

Do not be afraid to move outside of your circle
or comfort zone to seek the help that you need.

Journal Questions:

- How do you typically look for help from God?

_____

_____

_____

_____

_____

_____

_____

_____

_____

- What issues have you had or do you have that no one in your friend
  or family zone can help you with?

_____

_____

_____

_____

_____

_____

_____

_____

_____

_____

- Who or what type of people should you be talking to about your specific challenges?

_____

_____

_____

_____

_____

_____

_____

_____

_____

_____

Prayer: Dear heavenly Father, please connect me with those whom You have assigned to help me through my process. Let me know that You have sent them, and let their words ring confirmation of Your direction. Help me not be afraid to speak with them as You put us together for Your purpose.

41

What Are Your Street Signs to Victory?

Thanks be to God, who gives us this victory through our Lord Jesus Christ! As a result of all this, my loved brothers and sisters, you must stand firm, unshakable, excelling in the work of the Lord, as always, because you know that your labor isn't going to be for nothing in the Lord.
—1 CORINTHIANS 15:57–58 (CEB)

Be on your guard and stay awake. Your enemy, the devil, is like a roaring lion, sneaking around to find someone to attack.
—1 PETER 5:8 (CEV)

While driving home, before arriving to your street, you pass other street signs along the way. You know that you are getting close to your destination when you are able to recognize those street signs that come before your street.

God has set us up to arrive at great destinations of victory. It's like we have been predestined to live on Victory Lane.

Just like with our drive home, there are typically signs or issues that we have to pass by before we reach our purposes. It's necessary to know that, when we see these signs or are faced with specific issues, Victory Lane is only a few streets ahead. Oftentimes, right before we reach our success, the devil will try to step in and devise a plan to delay our progress. Because he is not creative, he will typically use the exact same people or situational issues with which we're closely and emotionally connected to distract and stop us from moving forward.

It's important that we identify our personal street signs to victory so that we are able to recognize them every time they pop up to prevent us from accomplishing our purposes. It might be Job Street, where an employer begins to create problems for no just reason; Child Street, dealing with a child whose behavior suddenly gets out of hand; or even Health Street, dealing with a flare-up that seems to come only during these times. We cannot afford to get stuck or stopped on these streets. Recognizing that these are usually temporary distractions will allow us to assess and deal with them differently and with less emotion while continuously walking toward our victory.

What's the Focus?

Pay attention to what the enemy uses to throw you off track
and delay your arrival to victory so that
you continue to push forward.

Journal Questions:

- What street signs, people, or situations usually flare up right before you get blessed (e.g., family, work, relationship, health)?

_____

_____

_____

_____

_____

_____

_____

_____

_____

- How can you prevent your own flare-ups or change your reactions?

_____

_____

_____

_____

_____

_____

_____

_____

_____

- What can you ask God to do regarding those street signs?

_____

_____

_____

_____

_____

_____

_____

_____

_____

Prayer: Dear heavenly Father, please keep me aware of those things that the enemy uses to annoy me and delay my process. Please show me how to deal with those things as they come and to become less emotional through the process.

42

Follow God to the End of Your Assignment!

The Lord said to Cyrus, His chosen one: I have taken hold
of your right hand to help you capture nations and remove
kings from power. City gates will open for you; not one will
stay closed. As I lead you, I will level mountains and break the
iron bars on bronze gates of cities. I will give you treasures
hidden in dark and secret places. Then you will know that
I, the Lord GOD of Israel, have called you by name.

—ISAIAH 45:1–3 (CEV)

Do not be afraid or discouraged, for the Lord will
personally go ahead of you. He will be with you;
He will neither fail you nor abandon you.

—DEUTERONOMY 31:8 (NLT)

When God reveals an assignment that He has for us to do, we're
often thrilled in the beginning just to have the opportunity to
work for God. Once we get started, however, it is easy to doubt our
ability to get the work finished.

Feeling discouraged and lost and questioning whether we have the
strength and power to open the doors that we'll need to walk through
in order to succeed is normal. However, when God chooses us for an
assignment, we have to remember that He will always complete His
work and that He said that He will hold our hands, level mountains,
pave the road, open gates, and make a way for us to move forward.

Now is *not* the time to be nervous about our next step. Now is the time to connect with God's strength and be brave in every step that we take from this point on, knowing that He has literally paved the ground in front of us so that each of our steps will be secure. Walking behind the King should give us the confidence to walk standing up straight, knowing that He will guide us with direction and protect us as we move along on our journeys.

What's the Focus?

If you walk right behind God, stay in communication
with Him, and move in His direction and pace,
you will complete your work at a level that only He can produce.

Journal Questions:

- What are you struggling to complete?

_____

_____

_____

_____

_____

_____

_____

_____

_____

- Do you feel that you are moving toward God's direction in your process or away from it?

_____

_____

_____

_____

_____

_____

_____

_____

_____

- What prevents you from walking directly behind God at times, and what do you believe can help you get closer to Him?

_____

_____

_____

_____

_____

_____

_____

_____

_____

Prayer: Dear heavenly Father, I thank You for considering me to be one of Your servants. Thank You for allowing me to work to help Your people and for trusting me enough to carry out Your assignments here on earth. I thank You for reminding me that You are with me at every step and that I do not have to be anxious, worried, discouraged, or afraid because You will never leave me.

43

When I Cross Your Mind,
Will You Pray for Me?

Here are my directions: Pray much for others;
plead for God's mercy upon them; give thanks
for all He is going to do for them.
—1 TIMOTHY 2:1 (TLB)

Every time you cross my mind, I break out in exclamations
of thanks to God. Each exclamation is a trigger to prayer.
I find myself praying for you with a glad heart.
—PHILIPPIANS 1:3–4 (MSG)

Praying for other people doesn't require a lot of our time or effort but is a very powerful thing to do. We don't always have time in our schedules to call, text, or email everyone when they cross our minds. We don't always have the time to physically connect with the people in our lives as much as we'd like. Connecting with others in person is great and makes us feel better, but connecting with them in the Spirit through prayer has the ability to make lives better.

As we take this journey to incorporate daily prayer for those in our lives, let's expand our coverage and exercise praying for those we do not know. Consider the grocery store clerks we see all the time, the young woman who is dressed provocatively and about whom we would normally speak negatively, the homeless man who is talking to himself, or the man who curses us out while driving next to us. What if a part of our job here on earth is to bring people who need help to God through prayer? Let's try replacing our normal reactions with quick prayers. This will not only help others but also help us to become more positive people who have a better perspective and closer relationship with God. God has blessed many of us with eyes to see, and we are to use our eyes to pay attention to those around us who need help.

What's the Focus?

When people come to mind,
have a conversation with God on their behalf.

Journal Questions:

- How often are you praying for others?

_____

_____

_____

_____

_____

_____

_____

_____

_____

_____

- During the day, how many times do you see people around you or think about your family or friends who are in distress?

_____

_____

_____

_____

_____

_____

_____

_____

_____

- What is your normal response to your thoughts about others in distress?

_____

_____

_____

_____

_____

_____

_____

_____

_____

Prayer: Dear heavenly Father, please help me to get into a habit of delivering my thoughts about others to You in prayer. Help me to realize that prayer does change situations and that I should be in constant conversation with you about the things I experience and hear about from others. Thank You, Lord, for allowing me to come to You for change, direction, and perspective.

44

What Are You Not Letting Go Of?

And my God shall supply all of your needs according
to HIS riches and glory by Christ Jesus.
—PHILIPPIANS 4:19 (NKJV)

What are you filling your hands (your life) with that makes them too full for God to hand you the blessings that are intended for you? God wants us to have what is best for our lives and will supply our every need, as written by Paul in Philippians 4:19. If you'll notice, the text says that He will supply our every *need* but does not refer to our every *want*. Oftentimes we grab onto so many things and ideas that we want for our lives while treating God's will as secondary advice or a mandatory pickup once we've gotten ourselves into a bad situation and can't do anything but watch Him work things out for us. Until we truly understand that we can never plan our lives' paths better than God already has, we will not be able to recognize that it is useless for us to do anything without Him. All we have to do is listen and be obedient as we move forward in the path that He has designed for us. We are often not able to receive or carry the blessings that God has for us because our hands are so full of our own desires.

What's the Focus?

To get the greatness of God's will in our lives,
we have to be willing to give up our own.

Journal Questions:

- What (relationship, job, house, lifestyle) are you holding onto even though it may be standing in the way of your breakthrough (i.e., God's blessing)?

- Do you realize that in order to put God first, you have to be *willing* to let everything else go?

- What do you need to experience in order to have a level of faith and trust in God that allows you to put Him and His ways first?

_____

_____

_____

_____

_____

_____

_____

_____

_____

_____

Prayer: Dear heavenly Father, please help me to develop a relationship with You that allows me to trust You at every turn. Help me to know Your voice so that I can get aligned with Your desires for my life. God, help me to have the strength to let go of every situation in my life that is holding a space for something for which You have a replacement.

45

Take the Time to Get Prequalified for Your Run

If any of you need wisdom, you should ask God, and it will be given to you. God is generous and won't correct you for asking.
—JAMES 1:5 (CEV)

In order to make sure that we will be able to make it to the finish line of our purposes, we have to take the time to get prequalified for our run. As exciting as it is to realize that God has prepared a course for us, we don't always make the best use of the time that is given to us to train or get as prepared as we can before the run begins. The secret to finishing the course is not running fast but being prepared for the entire process.

When participating in a marathon, runners start training for the road ahead as soon as they find out about the run. They take the time to exercise and strengthen their muscles, eat right, take vitamins, drink plenty of water, and get plenty of rest because they understand that, except for a few quick breaks along the course, they will not have the time to prepare once the run has begun. The same thing often applies to the run that God has prepared for us. We are not supposed to rush through the process. God will often show us the finish line of a particular run that we are to complete but take us through multiple projects or tracks that will prepare us for what's to come. We are not supposed to get upset or frustrated about all the work between the promise that He gives and our arrival to the promised land. We are, however, expected to be happy to sit with God and prepare for every leg of the course.

What's the Focus?

The training (extra projects, experiences,
etc.) that God has aligned with
your assignment is a sign that you are being prepared for success.

Journal Questions:

- What is a promise or vision that you've received (a job promotion, new home, spouse) in the past that developed into reality?

_____

_____

_____

_____

_____

_____

_____

_____

_____

- What challenges or experiences did you deal with that served as training to help you maintain your blessing that occurred between the time you first received the vision and the moment you received the actual promise (e.g., being forced to work in a different position before getting your promotion, going through a mandatory financial management class, dating the wrong person in order to appreciate the right person)?

_____

_____

_____

_____

_____

_____

_____

_____

_____

_____

- What's the hardest part of waiting through the training period, and what can you do to make your training periods easier for you to deal with?

_____

_____

_____

_____

_____

_____

_____

_____

_____

_____

Prayer: Dear heavenly Father, thank You for taking the time to prepare me for Your greatness. I am so grateful that You not only have a plan for success for my life but that You have made sure that, through a series of training sessions, I will be ready, strong enough, and receptive to the blessings when they arrive.

46

Put a Period on It

So be careful how you act; these are difficult days. Don't
be fools; be wise: make the most of every opportunity
you have for doing good. Don't act thoughtlessly but try
to find out and do whatever the Lord wants you to.
—EPHESIANS 5:15–17 (TLB)

At some point we must learn how to put a period on, or end,
certain conversations and situations that are brought into our
lives. Oftentimes, we allow our minds to be consumed by the thought
of fixing problems that have not been assigned to us by God. We think
about these things over and over or have circular conversations about
these matters with no real resolution because we were never given
the power to provide the solution. Ultimately, these issues can be a
distraction from what God actually expects us to be doing. When we
linger in troubles that we are supposed to push past, we waste the time
that has been allotted for our lives. Knowing that the time that has
been given to us actually belongs to God should help us to understand
that, when we step outside of our daily assignment, we are really
wasting God's time. When we understand that everything we allow
to come into our daily plan should be for a purpose, it becomes easier
to start filtering through what we do or don't have time for.

We must learn how to assess each situation with which we are faced,
determine what our personal position is in the matter (if any), and
decide how we're supposed to deal with the situation. When we are
not meant to be the solution, we have to learn how to put a period on

the conversation or situation and move forward. We can't spend more of our time talking about the distractions in our lives than working to plant the seeds of our purposes.

What's the Focus?

End conversations and situations that are
not assigned to you by God.

Journal Questions:

- What conversations or situations are you dealing with that you would really like to end or get out of?

_____

_____

_____

_____

_____

_____

_____

_____

_____

_____

- What do you feel you may risk by pulling yourself out of the scenario?

_____

_____

_____

_____

_____

_____

_____

_____

_____

- Have you asked God to give you the words to excuse yourself from this issue?

_____

_____

_____

_____

_____

_____

_____

_____

_____

Prayer: Dear heavenly Father, please make my words and positioning clear in every situation that I am brought into. Give me the clarity and strength to pull away from situations that have nothing to do with Your purpose for my life. Give me the confidence to speak in the direction of Your will.

47

What Are You Willing to Go through in Order to Get through to Someone Else?

The Lord wants to use you for special purposes,
so make yourself clean from all evil. Then
you will be holy, and the Master can use you.
You will be ready for any good work.
—2 TIMOTHY 2:21(ERV)

You must each decide in your heart how much to give.
And don't give reluctantly or in response to pressure.
"For God loves a person who gives cheerfully."
—2 CORINTHIANS 9:7 (NLT)

I f we look at our lives as vessels that God uses to push temporary assignments through, it changes our perspective of how we see the tests and trials that we are faced with. When God has a lesson for us to learn, it's important to remember that, in a vessel, the blood runs through the vein but is going somewhere else.

The same thing applies to the lessons and wisdom given to us from God. When God allows us to go through an experience, good or bad, it is typically something that we will be led to share with others at some point in our lives. Even though God could speak His words directly through us, He will often take the time to train, prepare, and put us on a personal journey through our assignments so that we can be a living example to others of how to live through what they're dealing with.

We don't know to whom our assignments will lead us. What we do know, however, is that just as a professional is trained for work, God will provide us with the training for the work that we are to carry out. Generally, our training to help someone else pass through his or her trial comes from our direct experience of having gone through that same circumstance. Although we want to be a vessel for God to help other people in theory, we would usually prefer not to have to go through something to get through to someone else. Unfortunately, it is impossible for us to grow in a way that we can be used as a vessel for others and stand in our comfort zone at the same time.

What's the Focus?

Use what you've gone through to teach someone else how to navigate through the same type of circumstances.

Journal Questions:

- What is something that you've struggled through but were able to complete successfully?

_____

_____

_____

_____

_____

_____

_____

_____

_____

- What scenario have you experienced that you found yourself later teaching someone else how to get through?

_____

_____

_____

_____

_____

_____

_____

_____

- What are three life lessons you can share with others on a regular basis?

_____

_____

_____

_____

_____

_____

_____

_____

Prayer: Dear heavenly Father, please help me to develop a proper perspective for the journey on which You are taking me. Help me to see how the things that I experience can be a blessing to other people as I share with them those things that I have learned by going through the process.

48

God's Work: Opportunity or Obligation?

Yes, it is God who is working in you. He helps you want to do what pleases Him, and He gives you the power to do it. Do everything without complaining or arguing.
—PHILIPPIANS 2:12–13 (ERV)

Sometimes when God shows us something specific that we are to do for Him as a part of our lives' purposes, our perspectives on the opportunity is slightly off center. For instance, we're often happy to say that we are "doing God's work" because it is something that He has led us to do, but we tend to look at it as more of an *obligation* rather than the *opportunity* that it is. We will sometimes say things like, "I have to do this because it is what God told me to do," rather than, "Let me tell you what God has given me the opportunity to be a part of." Having proper perspective is the key that will open our minds to a different level of understanding, happiness, and peacefulness, which will ultimately prevent us from complaining and being stressed about tasks that we should be happy to have been selected to carry out. The scripture reminds us that God helps us do what pleases Him and that He will give us the power to complete the process. Therefore, we will be successful and do not have to complain.

We must consider as we are deciding when we will start doing His work that His opportunities are associated with appointed times. When we receive His confirmation of an assignment, we have to begin by asking the right questions that will help us to move forward, like, "When should I start?" "Whom have You chosen to work with me on this?" and "Is there anything specific that I need to know before moving forward?" When we are grateful for our opportunities, we are more likely to be used on a regular basis.

What's the Focus?

Always remember that it is an opportunity
to carry out any work on behalf of the Lord.

Journal Questions:

- What is the last thing that you were asked to do that you complained about (i.e., sighed, made a negative comment about)?

_____

_____

_____

_____

_____

_____

_____

_____

_____

_____

- How does it make you feel when someone does something for you strictly out of an obligation and not because he or she is genuinely happy to do it?

_____

_____

_____

_____

_____

_____

_____

_____

_____

- When was the last time you looked for opportunities to serve God in your daily walk (e.g., by helping someone on the street, creating a project that will benefit others)?

_____

_____

_____

_____

_____

_____

_____

_____

_____

Prayer: Dear heavenly Father, please bless me with opportunities to work for You and the mindset to do Your work in the right spirit. I want to be used by You here on earth as one of Your representatives. I want to be unstressed and able to carry out my assignments. I know, however, that in order to do so, I have to have the proper perspective and understanding. Please continue to remind me that You have already given me the power necessary to succeed in all that You have planned and that I should do my work without arguing or complaining. Help me to be joyous in this work so that I will be a reflection to others of how wonderful it is to work for You so that they will want to work for You as well.

49

A Paper Is Written for the Benefit of the Student, Not the Teacher

Joyful is the person who finds wisdom, the one who gains understanding. For wisdom is more profitable than silver, and her wages are better than gold. Wisdom is more precious than rubies; nothing you desire can compare with her.
—PROVERBS 3:13–15 (NLT)

When writing papers, students might feel as though they are doing the work for the benefit of their teacher. We hear students say, "I have to turn this paper in for my professor." This mindset often carries over into how we relate to God when He has something for us to prepare for our journeys ahead.

When God has something for us, He preapproves it before He accepts our paperwork. Although we have preapproval from God, we are still required to go through the exercise of gathering our thoughts, researching facts, and writing everything down for the benefit of our own understanding. This process that He takes us through prepares us so that when we're ready to present the idea in a public arena, we have an excellent understanding of what we are presenting and will have become educated as we have been accelerated to the next level.

God is not asking us to "turn our paper in" (or prepare, train, and experience specific things along the way) because He needs to read it but because we need to have a very good understanding about the subject at hand before we move onto the next level of where He would have us be.

What's the Focus?

Embrace what God has you doing in times of preparation,
as it is to get you ready for your journey ahead.

Journal Questions:

- What have you been forced to prepare for recently (e.g., a job, buying a house)?

_____

_____

_____

_____

_____

_____

_____

_____

_____

_____

- How did you prepare your mindset to get through what you needed to do?

_____

_____

_____

_____

_____

_____

_____

_____

_____

_____

- How open are you to being challenged in mandatory situations?

_____

_____

_____

_____

_____

_____

_____

_____

_____

Prayer: Dear heavenly Father, please help me to be more joyful when seeking wisdom. Help me to understand that preparation is a part of a process that You use to place me into my position successfully.

50

What Is the Budget without the Training?

Seek the Kingdom of God above all else, and
He will give you everything you need.
—LUKE 12:31 (NLT)

God can bless you with everything you need, and you will always
have more than enough to do all kinds of good things for others.
—2 CORINTHIANS 9:8 (CEV)

When we offer our lives to God and make ourselves available to complete the work that He has set for us to accomplish, we are then signing up to work for the world's best employer. There are different types of assignments that will add up to our lives' purposes and many stages that we will go through in order to fulfill each project.

A factor that we are often faced with when dealing with any project is the budget. In our planning process we have to consider the big picture and how much it will cost to complete the task. It can be challenging to hear from God, see His vision, be obedient, and carry out the steps but not have the money to finalize the work. People often say when they are faced with this situation that they feel as though God has them at a standstill. God will use this time while we're standing still to train us on how we are to use His budget so that after He has given us the money, we do not misuse the funds. If we worked for any other employer and there was a budget attached to our assignment, the money would be released only after the employer felt confident that we had been properly trained and had a clear understanding on how the budget was to be distributed. God will allow us, if we listen, to sit in training with Him until we completely understand how His budget is to be spent according to His purpose. We must continue to pray, asking God to train and show us how to effectively carry out His work.

What's the Focus?

Spend time with God and ask Him how
He wants you to allocate funds
before you ask Him to send them.

Journal Questions:

* How much money do you need for your next project?

_____

_____

_____

_____

_____

_____

_____

_____

_____

_____

_____

- Have you mapped out a full plan for your proposed budget?

_____
_____
_____
_____
_____
_____
_____
_____

- Have you consulted with God to find out if He has any changes?

_____
_____
_____
_____
_____
_____
_____
_____

Prayer: Dear heavenly Father, thank You for the vision to carry out Your work. Please show me how to draft a budget that will cover all the expenses necessary to do this work. Let me not ask for too little so that when we need to execute Your plans we are without the proper resources to move forward. Let me be a great steward over all that You provide for me to manage. Help me to understand where every dollar is to be spent and why it should be allocated in the way that You have outlined.

51

Who Supplies Your Needs?

The Lord is near to everyone who sincerely calls to Him for help.
—PSALM 145:18 (ERV)

The Bible states that God will supply *all* our needs. However, many say that we should only ask God for help with certain things. They say that we should not bother Him with other issues because He could use that time to solve bigger problems in the world.

The Bible does not say that we should only talk with Him about things that are considered to be important by human standards. Those types of boundaries are set by the devil in an effort to discourage us from building a greater relationship with God. Once we have developed a relationship with God where we find ourselves having conversations with Him throughout the day, we begin to understand that we should take all our concerns to Him because He truly supplies all our needs. This does not mean that we will receive everything that we ask for. It means that He will listen to and give us the direction that we need according to His purpose. The devil would like for us to think that we should figure things out by ourselves because God is too busy. The moment that we buy into that belief is when we will begin to look for someone else to guide us, and it becomes the perfect opportunity for the devil to send the wrong person or solution to "help" with our problem. The Bible reminds us that we can do *all* things through Christ who strengthens us and that He will supply all our needs. We should not feel that we are bothering God by talking to Him but should talk to Him about everything that we do and then listen and look for His guidance and direction toward the right solutions.

What's the Focus?

Go to God with every thought, question, and proposal first because it is He who assigns the right people to help us.

Journal Questions:

- Who do you typically talk to first when you need something?

_____
_____
_____
_____
_____
_____
_____
_____
_____
_____

- When you talk to God are you typically just looking for a yes or are you open to a conversation with Him beyond His approval?

_____
_____
_____
_____
_____
_____
_____
_____
_____
_____
_____
_____

- How can you improve your relationship with God through your conversations?

_____

_____

_____

_____

_____

_____

_____

_____

_____

Prayer: Dear heavenly Father, thank You for offering to provide my every need. Thank You, Father, for being available every time that I need to talk about anything. Please help me to remember that when I feel alone, You are there to hear my every thought, comfort me along the way, and offer guidance as I move forward.

52

Are You Paying Attention to What You're Going through or Just Going through It?

We often suffer, but we are never crushed. Even when we don't know what to do, we never give up. In times of trouble, God is with us, and when we are knocked down, we get up again.
—2 CORINTHIANS 4:8–9 (CEV)

I will show you and teach you in the way you should go.
I will tell you what to do with my eye upon you.
—PSALM 32:8 (NLT)

Many of us seem to be personally going through or subjected to something that is tiresome and leaves us feeling as though we are living in survival mode. When looking to the Bible for guidance, we are reminded in 2 Corinthians 4:8 that God is with us during our times of trouble and that although we may be down, we will get up again. Knowing this should help us understand that there is a purpose to everything that is happening.

We have to mentally put our trials into three separate categories: distractions, lessons, and action items. Distractions become easier to detect over time because they typically have no lesson attached to them. God will often allow them to be placed in our lives, especially before He is about to promote us, in order to see if we're focused enough to handle the distractions that will come to us at the next level. Many of our experiences are lessons that we are supposed to learn from and become able to lead others past later down the road. Action items require that we stop and become the help that is necessary to solve the problem that we are facing. Everything is supposed to be for purpose. We were never intended to just go through the motions of a situation; instead, we are to pay attention to why we've been positioned in a particular place so that we can move God's plans forward.

What's the Focus?
Pay special attention to what you're going
through so that you can identify its
purpose and the proper time that should be
spent dealing with the situation.

Journal Questions:

- What is the most trying thing that you have gone through recently?

_____

_____

_____

_____

_____

_____

_____

_____

_____

_____

- Looking at it now, was it a distraction, a personal lesson, or an action item?

_____

_____

_____

_____

_____

_____

_____

_____

_____

_____

- How can you better allot your time by categorizing what it is that you are going through?

_____

_____

_____

_____

_____

_____

_____

_____

_____

Prayer: Dear heavenly Father, please help me to see things clearly as they are coming toward me. Help me to identify the purpose of the circumstances that I am faced with so that I can better allot my time and attention to what is actually happening and set my plans accordingly.

Scripture Glossary

1. **Make Your Reservations and God Will Buy Your Ticket.**
   a. Philippians 1:6 (Common English Version)

2. **Is It Harder to Sit Still in a Moment of Patience or Walk on a Rocky Road?**
   a. Psalm 37:23 (Common English Version)

3. **Walk Through and See Who's at the Door to Help You. It May Not Be Who You Think.**
   a. Proverbs 3:5 (Common English Version)

4. **Sometimes It Takes a Tornado to Move Us Into the Right Location.**
   a. Genesis 50:20 (Common English Bible)

5. **Are You Pressing the Snooze Button on Your Alarm Clock With God?**
   a. Ecclesiastes 3:1 (Easy-to-Read Version)

6. **What Kind of Fruit Do People Pick From You?**
   a. Luke 6:43-49 (Common English Version)
   b. Ephesians 4:29 (New International Version)

7. **Can God Add More to Your Life or Are You "Just Working Here?"**
   a. 2 Timothy 2:15 (Living Bible)

8. **A Miracle Cannot Be Contained in a Box.**
   a. 1 Chronicles 16:12 (New Living Translation)
   b. 1 Corinthians 2:9 (Easy-to-Read Version)

9. **Do Not Let Doubt Be a Tumor That Kills Your Faith.**
   a. Matthew 21:21-22 (Easy-to-Read Version)

10. **Let This Scene Play Through.**
    a.   Psalm 37:5 (Contemporary English Version)

11. **Pay Attention to What God Is Showing You**
    a.   Jeremiah 29:11 (Common English Bible)
    b.   John 14:25-26 (Contemporary English Version)

12. **Surround Yourself With People Who Remind You to Have Great Posture.**
    a.   Proverbs 13:20 (New Life Version)
    b.   1 Corinthians 15:33 (New Life Version)

13. **Allow God to be Your Life's Preserver.**
    a.   Isaiah 43:2 (New Living Translation)
    b.   Romans 10:13 (Living Bible)

14. **Do Not Extend Contracts That God Has Not Signed Off On.**
    a.   Psalm 18:30 (Easy-to-Read Version)

15. **How Long Will You Praise Before You Complain?**
    a.   Isaiah 65:24 (Living Bible)
    b.   Isaiah 41:17 (New International Version)

16. **Do Not Let An Impulse Destroy God's Plans For Your Life.**
    a.   Psalm 37:8 (The Message)
    b.   Psalm 37:34 (Living Bible)

17. **How Can You Pass the Class If You Will Not Prepare for the Test?**
    a.   1 Peter 5:6 (Living Bible)
    b.   1 Peter 5:10-11 (Living Bible)

18. **If We Put Ourselves in a Race With Everyone Else, We Will Have to Compete in Everyone Else's Race.**
    a.   Galatians 6:4-5 (New Life Version)
    b.   Romans 12:2 (Living Bible)

19. **What Are You Sewing Into Your Life?**
    a. Galatians 6:7-9 (The Message)
    b. Romans 12:2 (Living Bible)

20. **Do Not Put Artificial Plants on Top of Planted Seeds.**
    a. Psalm 1:2-4 (New Life Version)

21. **Allow God to Set the Stage for Your Performance.**
    a. Proverbs 16:3 (The Message)

22. **Everyone Cannot Swim on Your Team.**
    a. 1 Corinthians 15:58 (Contemporary English Version)
    b. Proverbs 27:17 (New Life Version)

23. **Are You Standing in the Middle of Your Miracle?**
    a. Isaiah 42:16 (Contemporary English Version)

24. **Never Fix a Vehicle That Has Been Totaled Out.**
    a. Psalm 73:24 (New International Version)
    b. Isaiah 43:18-19 (Easy-to-Read Version)

25. **Are You Willing to Live in "Fast Forward"?**
    a. Isaiah 48:17 (Easy-to-Read Version)

26. **Are You Ready to Get Picked Up?**
    a. Luke 12:35-36 (New International Version)
    b. Hebrews 11:7 (New Life Version)
    c. Ephesians 2:10 (Easy-to-Read Version)

27. **God's Will VS. Free "Wheel"**
    a. Romans 12:1 (Easy-to-Read Version)

28. **Where is Your Route (Or Life) Leading Others?**
    a. 1 Peter 5:3 (Easy –to-Read Version)

29. **Are Your Words Driving You Into the Wrong Direction?**
    a. Ephesians 4:29 (New American Standard Bible)
    b. Matthew 12:36 (Easy-to-Read Version)

30. **Don't Be Discouraged by the Size of Your Seed.**
    a. Matthew 13:31-32 (Living Bible)

31. **Allow Yourself to be Deeply Rooted.**
    a. Isaiah 40:31 (New Life Version)
    b. Philippians 2:13 (Common English Bible)

32. **It's Impossible to Shop in the Devil's Store and Come Out With God's Will.**
    a. Luke 6:46 (Contemporary English Version)
    b. Luke 16:13 (English Standard Version)

33. **Are You Looking Both Ways When Coming to a Stop Sign?**
    a. Isaiah 28:23 (New Life Version)
    b. John 10:27 (Living Bible)

34. **Be Prepared to Sharpen Your Pencil.**
    a. 1 Peter 4:12 (Contemporary English Version)

35. **What Are You Claiming in God's Name?**
    a. Exodus 3:13-15 (Contemporary English Version)
    b. Proverbs 18:21 (Contemporary English Version)

36. **Do Not Delay Your Delivery.**
    a. Romans 8:18-19 (Contemporary English Version)

37. **God Does Not Need Us For Every Part of the Plan.**
    a. Psalm 50:11-12, 14 (Contemporary English Version)

38. **What Are You Putting Into Your Pockets?**
    a. Psalm 32:8 (New Living Translation)

39. **Check Your Oxygen Level.**
    a. Acts 17:25 (Contemporary English Version)

40. **Be Careful About Taking Directions From Someone Who Has Not Been Where You're Going.**
    a. Psalm 20:2 (Contemporary English Version)

41. **What Are Your Street Signs to Victory?**
    a. 1 Corinthians 15:57-58 (Common English Bible)
    b. 1 Peter 5:8 (Contemporary English Version)

42. **Follow God to the End of Your Assignment.**
    a. Isaiah 45:1-3 (Contemporary English Version)
    b. Deuteronomy 31:8 (New Living Translation Version)

43. **When I Cross Your Mind, Will You Pray For Me?**
    a. 1 Timothy 2:1 (Living Bible)
    b. Philippians 1:3-4 (The Message)

44. **What Are You Not Letting Go Of?**
    a. Philippians 4:19 (New King James Version)

45. **Take the Time to Get Prequalified for Your Run.**
    a. James 1:5 (Contemporary English Version)

46. **Put a Period on It.**
    a. Ephesians 5:15-17 (Living Bible)

47. **What Are You Willing to Go Through in Order to Get Through To Someone Else?**
    a. 2 Timothy 2:21 (Easy-to-Read Version)
    b. 2 Corinthians 9:7 (New Living Translation)

48. **God's Work: Opportunity or Obligation?**
    a. Philippians 2:12-13 (Easy-to-Read Version)

49. **A Paper is Written for the Benefit for the Student, Not for the Benefit of the Teacher.**
    a. Proverbs 3:13-15 (New Living Translation)

50. **What is Budget Without the Training?**
    a. Luke 12:31 (New Living Translation)
    b. 2 Corinthians 9:8 (Contemporary English Version)

51. **Who Supplies Your Needs?**
    a. Psalm 145:18 (Easy-to-Read Version)

52. **Are You Paying Attention to What You You're Going Through or Just Going Through It?**
    a. 2 Corinthians 4:8-9 (Contemporary English Version)

About the Author

BeNeca Griffin is a Christian Author, International Speaker and Branding Specialist who is active in spreading the Word of GOD. As a Branding Specialist she works with Fortune 100/500 companies, seasoned executives, entrepreneurs, universities, young adults and high school students in an effort to help them develop their individual thumbprint in the business of their life's purpose. Her company Moments of Focus LLC is centered on developing purpose driven content, services and products. She was recognized by the White House in 2010 as a Community Leader. Her book 3rd Generation Country, a Practical Guide to Raising Children with Great Values was nominated for an NAACP Image Award.

Printed in the United States
By Bookmasters